PEAK
PERFORMANCE
CULTURE

PEAK
PERFORMANCE
CULTURE

THE FIVE METRICS OF

ORGANIZATIONAL EXCELLENCE

DAVE MITCHELL

WILEY

Published by John Wiley & Sons, Inc., Hoboken, New Jersey.

Published simultaneously in Canada.

For general information on our other products and services or for technical support, please contact our Customer Care Department within the United States at (800) 762-2974, outside the United States at (317) 572-3993 or fax (317) 572-4002.

Wiley publishes in a variety of print and electronic formats and by print-on-demand. Some material included with standard print versions of this book may not be included in e-books or in print-on-demand. If this book refers to media such as a CD or DVD that is not included in the version you purchased, you may download this material at http://booksupport.wiley.com. For more information about Wiley products, visit www.wiley.com.

Library of Congress Cataloging-in-Publication Data

Names: Mitchell, Dave, 1961- author.
Title: Peak performance culture : the five metrics of organizational
   excellence / Dave Mitchell.
Description: Hoboken, New Jersey : John Wiley & Sons, Inc., [2020] |
   Includes bibliographical references and index.
Identifiers: LCCN 2020025504 (print) | LCCN 2020025505 (ebook) | ISBN
   9781119581499 (hardback) | ISBN 9781119581512 (adobe pdf) | ISBN
   9781119581505 (epub)
Subjects: LCSH: Organizational effectiveness. | Organizational behavior. |
   Corporate culture. | Performance.
Classification: LCC HD58.9 .M567 2020 (print) | LCC HD58.9 (ebook) | DDC
   658.3/14—dc23
LC record available at https://lccn.loc.gov/2020025504
LC ebook record available at https://lccn.loc.gov/2020025505

Cover design: Wiley

Printed in the United States of America

SKY10020251_080320

Contents

Preface

I didn't see that coming.

It was January 2012. Verona, Italy. My 16-plus years (at that time) as an international speaker on organizational development did not prepare me for what I was about to experience. The 12 years I'd worked in corporate human resources development before *that* also failed me. Nothing about the chain of events leading up to this moment foretold the incredible reveal that would happen at an auditorium within a vibrant pharmaceutical research and manufacturing facility.

The day had started as normal as a day can start when you grew up in a small town in southern Illinois and find yourself in an incredible Italian city surrounded by the architecture, culture, and lore that Verona offers. Only a few blocks from my hotel was "Juliet's House" – Verona was the setting for Shakespeare's *Romeo and Juliet*.

The day before, my lovely bride and I had toured the city on our own. Particularly memorable was the arena. It wasn't hard to imagine gladiators competing within this incredible amphitheater, the third largest in all of Italy. One of my favorite photos is a shot that Lori took of me on the "playing field" of the arena, having just sculpted "Maximus Dave" in the sand with my feet. We walked around several piazzas, visited museums, and essentially maintained an unsurpassed sense of awe all day.

Me at the arena in Verona, Italy.

But this day had started normally. It was training day. Whether the event is in Verona or Detroit, my preparation is the same. There was the usual breakfast at the hotel, laptop to be packed up, and a car to transport me to the site exactly as expected. We traversed Verona, leaving the history of the city center for the modernity of the industrial district.

Gaining access to a pharmaceutical facility – especially one that both conducts cutting-edge research and produces large volumes of drugs – is not simple. Having done an event in Langley, Virginia, for the CIA, I am no stranger to security protocols. Suffice it to say, this site was more secure than our icon of the intelligence community. After providing ample evidence of my identity and receiving my badge clearly labeling me as VISITOR (a wholly unnecessary label given my obvious confusion and distinct American pronunciation when struggling through Italian greetings), I made my way through the labyrinth of gates, doors, and hallways necessary to access the learning center.

Today my audience would be scientists – 400 highly educated experts in the field of chemistry. Most of the attendees would be Italian, but there were representatives from all over the world. I was focused on the delivery of my content. I describe my public speaking style as "enter-train-ment," and humor plays a large role in my presentations. I have been described as the unlikely pitch cross of a college psychology teacher who moonlights as a stand-up comic. My seminar that day was *Consultative Selling: The Customer Centric Sale*. Much of the content was derived from my most popular program, *The Power of Understanding People*. I was anxious about how the material would translate. Would my humor work for this audience? Scientists, multicultural visitors, potential language barriers – these are the things that keep training professionals up at night.

As the crowd began to assemble, I tried to mitigate my nervousness by mingling with the attendees. Perhaps some schmoozing of the crowd would allay my fears, I thought. It didn't. Despite my attempts to learn a few words in Italian, I quickly felt awkward during most interactions. Beyond the language challenges, I was certain that this group of analytical, detailed, and fact-based professionals had little interest in something so conceptual as consultative selling. It was not like I hadn't worked with pharmaceutical companies before; I had, many times. But it was almost always with sales professionals. This was a different demographic. In my nomenclature, these were Experts – a way of thinking that is based on pragmatic best practices gathered from personal experience. Things that you can *know* to be true. "What on earth would a scientist care about this topic?" I thought to myself. It is entirely theoretical.

It was also not like I hadn't experienced this kind of crowd before. In my seminars, I often share the story of presenting to chemical engineers in Lake Jackson, Texas – a memory that has traumatized me for 20 years. Essentially, it was three hours of me feverishly attempting to elicit some type of reaction from 35 stoic audience members, only to ultimately fail. It still haunts me, even though my client tells me that the attendees that day still talk about that seminar. "Me, too," I reply.

On stage in Verona, my host introduced me with the bio that I had provided. Two years later, *The Power of Understanding People* would be released as a critically acclaimed book, but I remember wishing for that kind of credibility in that moment. As I made my way to the stage, my mind raced with toxic thoughts. I like to start strong with some mildly self-deprecating humor, but I worried that it would be lost in translation. How would I react to a crowd that didn't laugh? Would I again escalate my energy to manic levels? I began reliving the mistakes of Lake Jackson, Texas. Oh, and did I mention that this was the first event of a week-long schedule of seminars? Imagine the emotional pain involved if I discovered in this first session that I was out of my element—for me *and* the crowd.

The first surprise struck me more as a sense of relief than insight. They laughed. They were engaged. It was the first clue to the larger reveal that was to come when they completed the interactive-style assessment about 45 minutes later. For the time being, I just felt the reassurance that this was going to go well and that all my fears had been for naught. While that was personally satisfying, the big revelation arrived when I asked the group to stand as I polled their interactive style results.

Readers of my last two books, *The Power of Understanding People* and *The Power of Understanding Yourself*, know that I discuss four iconic ways of communicating:

The Expert: Detailed, fact-based, thorough

The Romantic: Emotional, tactful, diplomatic

The Mastermind: Conceptual, systemic, unpredictable

The Warrior: Logical, direct, results oriented

I fully expected most of the room to rise when I introduced the Expert style. In fact, only a handful of attendees stood. Same for the Warrior and Mastermind styles. More than 75% of the room would score as a Romantic.

"What? How can this be?" I thought to myself. How is it that these incredibly knowledgeable chemists, technicians, and researchers would be so emotionally sensitive? It had not occurred to me that these professionals were not merely drawn to the science of health care, but also to the service of others.

It was at this moment that I knew that the organization had a core ideology that could differentiate it from its competitors. This corporate culture was unique, possessing not just the technical expertise to enhance the work of those clients whom they supported, but also a passion for helping others. We already knew they had a head for science, but we discovered that day that they also had a heart for service.

And so it was that the company's core ideology was discovered. "Heads for Science, Hearts for Service" became their brand – the basis for horizontal and vertical alignment. The entire organization – with locations in England, Scotland, Italy, and the United States – began the process of implementing an operational and marketing strategy around this ideology. And it all started with the realization that they had something special in their culture. Something that would resonate with the marketplace and produce successful fiscal results. It was just a starting point toward peak performance, but a necessary one.

This book is about just that: recognizing and leveraging your organization's "special sauce." It is about creating an infrastructure that maximizes the strength of the institution, both employee facing and customer facing. It is about separating your operation from those of your competitors. It is about building an organization of peak performance, much like you would build a house: with a foundation, framework, and power sources to create something special for its inhabitants.

There is a lot of information in this book. One of my favorite attendees and loyal readers messaged me after my last book saying, "I am enjoying your new book, but it is much denser than your previous book. There is a lot to consider." This book increases that density. In a way, it completes the trinity of my work involving of cognitive and organizational psychology spanning nearly a decade, a trifecta including understanding yourself, others, and the organization. We are going on a journey to every corner of the organization, from the proverbial 40,000-foot view to the minutiae of policies. There are ideas, strategies, tactics, best practices, assessments, checklists, and examples to illustrate the full range of organizational development considerations – all designed to assist the reader in building a higher-performing institution.

This book is about peak performance culture. It is about operational excellence. It is about finding and delivering – every single time, every single day – your own secret sauce.

Acknowledgments

This book is the product of interactions with countless leaders, specifiers, influencers, and team members of thousands of organizations with whom I am proud to have worked. Since founding the Leadership Difference, Inc. it has been my great fortune to travel the world – not just to educate, but more importantly to be educated. Thank you, all of you who have made the last 25 years so amazing.

As I am writing this book, the world is experiencing a generational event – the COVID-19 pandemic. Great organizations will lead us out of this challenge and into a period of new progress, prosperity, and innovation, largely due to their own operational excellence and peak performance cultures. I look forward to watching it happen. We will persevere and transcend.

For the last 35 years, my lovely bride, Lori, is my reason for being. It bears repeating (as I mentioned in my previous book) that you never stop astounding me as a person, a spouse, a mother, and a friend. I love you more than I thought it possible to love. We quarantined together during the pandemic and didn't really notice anything different in our behaviors. Turns out, we have been self-isolating with each other all along.

All my love to my daughter, Brooke; my son, Slade; my sister, Diana; Debby, Nancy, Russ, Tom, and Peggy.

A shout out to the best editors a writer could have, Vicki Adang and Christine Moore.

Those who know me best know that I have a special affinity for my dogs. Since my last book, we adopted Mingus. He is 130 pounds of Irish wolfhound and border collie. He taught me that small, smart dogs are good; big, dumb dogs are good; but big, smart dogs are a problem. We have locked our cabinets and refrigerator; duct taped our sectional, and reinforced all fences. And when I would get frustrated with the world, it was Mingus who would drop a ball at my feet and run in the direction he wanted it thrown. It was his reminder to me that when things get tough, grab the ball and start running with a purpose.

Peak Performance Culture

Introduction

By 1981, it had become clear that a debilitating lack of talent was likely to create a ceiling for my baseball career well below the major leagues. So it was, after my sophomore year of college, that I needed to choose a major. Since I had worked part-time at a commercial radio station – shout out to WCRA/WCRC FM in Effingham, Illinois—and the closed-circuit radio station on the college campus at Eastern Illinois University, I decided that Mass Communications would make the most sense. Heck, I might well become a sportscaster, the next best thing to nabbing the first baseman position for the New York Mets (my original occupational aspiration). My guidance counselor concurred but offered one suggestion. Given that I had a highgrade point average and appeared to arrive at my academic major largely based on convenience rather than aptitude, she encouraged me to augment my Mass Comm major with a business administration minor. You know, just in case my sportscasting career went the way of my baseball career.

When my broadcasting career fizzled – turns out the guidance counselor was on to something – I found myself without a clear idea about my professional future. I bounced around for a year – a very interesting year that you really should ask me about if we are having a glass of wine together. Eventually, I ended up in Chicago and working in retail. About six months into a job as a customer service representative – a job that essentially meant that you got yelled at by angry people for 8 hours and then went home to a frozen dinner alone in a roach-infested apartment (but I don't want to romanticize it), a position as a trainer opened up. My first job in human resources development was teaching new hires how to use the point of sale system at Marshall Field's. I loved it.

The job was hard. I led eight-hour training sessions on highly repetitive tasks. It wasn't sexy, or fun. At least it wasn't for most people, but it was for me. I still remember meetings with other store trainers during the holiday season hiring blitz. They all had the same look: dead eyes, expressionless face, shuffling gate, garbled muttering under their breath that sounded vaguely like a countdown until Thanksgiving—the unofficial end date of the seasonal hiring. Not me, however. I couldn't wait to get up in front of a new class, memorize their names, beguile them with stories of how to navigate a credit card sale to be shipped out of state as a gift to a third party using an American Express card. Good times. I had found my passion.

Unfortunately, I became the epitome of the "Peter Principle" – Laurence Peter's observation that people tend to get promoted until they reach their level of incompetence. I find Laurence's observations a little constrictive. I think the Peter Principle is broader than reaching a level of incompetence. I think many people simply reach a level of disinterest. After over a decade of promotions within the field of human resources development, I had reached an executive level that was entirely about strategies, budgets, staffing, and litigation defense. The area of passion that ignited my career – training and education – was nary a part of my last corporate job. I knew I needed to realign my profession with my joy.

"FAT ENOUGH, HAPPY ENOUGH" ISN'T ENOUGH

In 1995, I left corporate America to pursue my muse: the Leadership Difference, Inc. Armed with a business plan and a passion for training and development, I envisioned myself providing high-level leadership development to small- and medium-sized companies that otherwise could not afford to have a full-time staff member dedicated to this role. That vision has evolved over the years; now I spend more time delivering keynote speeches than seminars. But the 25 years since has given me a glimpse – sometimes more – into the vagaries that constitute "organizational culture."

In 1995, the concept of corporate culture was just finding an audience in the business world. It had existed for around 30 years – largely as an academic construct – but had become more popular as an organizational development consideration in the 1980s and 1990s. It was still a bit of an enigma – one that continues to this day. What exactly *is* a "culture"? More importantly, what kind of culture drives peak performance? Finally, how do I create a peak performance culture?

That's the challenge.

As an aside, there is an important lesson in my own company's evolution. It began with a vision to be the training and development partner to other organizations. Providing education is my passion. That passion supplied the fuel to begin my organization, but that alone would not be enough to sustain it. Much of what follows in this book is a map for harnessing and directing passion in a way that will achieve success. Without passion, there can be no success; but passion without structure is a recipe for failure. I see that every day in business. That is an important thing to understand about a peak performance culture. Culture is not entirely conceptual. It requires that you combine concept with execution, principles with practices, vision with pragmatism.

Interestingly, it may not be the best organizations from which I have learned the most. Most of the companies and associations I have been exposed to do not apply the best practices outlined in this book. The truth is, even relatively successful organizations are plodding along, using processes that hamstring their success. It is a variation of the "no news is good news" mentality in that they have managed to do things just good enough to have success that is just good enough. Perhaps the better cliché is "fat and happy." Or maybe "fat enough and happy enough." But fat enough and happy enough do not allow you to achieve a peak performance culture.

For example, in preparation for a speaking engagement, I like to schedule a phone call with the key contact(s) to better understand their goals for the session. Minimally, I like to know the demographics of the audience and how they will benefit by and apply the concepts that I will be sharing. Optimally, I would like to integrate my content within the broader context of the conference at large or the strategies of the organization. This exercise is a version of "horizontal alignment," a concept that will be explained later in the book. Peak performance culture requires broad vision, strategies, and ideologies designed to connect the needs of the market with the measures of organizational success.

Most of my clients are eager to provide at least a minimal amount of information for this purpose. Now, that sounds hopeful, but consider for a moment the fact that a significant percentage of my clients don't take the time to educate a guest speaker on information that will make the transfer of learning easier and enhance the likelihood of the attendees actually applying new and useful skills. That is a bit shocking to me. Add to that fact that only a handful of clients each year take the time to help me understand their current strategic approach, and how I can and should align with that during my presentation. I don't think this is an oversight of communication so much as a lack of clarity on that strategy. Many conferences don't have a clear purpose, desired outcomes, or even a theme.

I am not sharing that to shame anyone. People are busy. Conferences and training seminars are often constructed from checklists rather than strategic plans. Location determined, check. Agenda created, check. Invites sent, check. Speaker hired, check. Hotel rooms reserved, check. Our lives are quickly enveloped by activities – "things to do" lists that seduce us into thinking we are working hard to achieve success. I am a box to be checked. This approach results in tons of tasks, but little attention to the event's purpose. Much of this work rhythm is created by the lack of the strong infrastructure described in this book. These events are not supporting some broader approach to peak performance so much as they are an annual event that the organization schedules because, well, we did one last year. Peak performance cultures are not just horizontally aligned, but also vertically aligned. This means that all the tasks within the organization are being performed for reasons that can be tracked back to the company's core vision, strategy, and ideology.

For example, a recent client approached me to do strategic planning facilitation. The group represented a local chapter of a national organization that is well known and established. To successfully facilitate the construction of a new strategy, I felt it would be beneficial for me to understand past strategic plans, the process they used to achieve them, and the usefulness these past efforts had on actual results. To that end, I met with the organization's executive director.

Turns out, the organization had *no* strategic plan and had never had one. They had a generic mission statement that was rarely referenced when conducting business. They didn't clearly define their measures of success, other than not to spend more money than they had. Again, this is common. To the credit of this organization, the new executive director and board wanted to change that. They realized that to achieve a peak performance culture, they would need a vision and a strategy that resonated with their market and a clear articulation of success (horizontal alignment). They also knew that this strategic plan would illuminate several actionable items necessary to achieve these goals (vertical alignment). Combine these two with passion, and you have a good start on a peak performance culture.

Again, my point is not to pass judgment on the leadership of organizations but rather to reassure you that most organizations are *not* applying the best practices outlined in this book. Why? Because organizational culture, let alone a peak performance version, is challenging to define. That's actually very good news. If an organization can survive without attending to the key metrics of peak performance, imagine the level of success they can aspire to if they *do* focus on these metrics. The trap many of these organizations fall into is that without the fear created by failure, they are often uninterested in doing the hard work – the visionary and strategic work, not the daily activities that keep you busy – necessary to unleash their full potential.

Passion, horizontal alignment, and vertical alignment are not the whole of peak performance culture, however. A comprehensive exploration of organizational culture must include the customer experience – because it is far less important to examine what *we* think our culture is compared to what our clients think. The employee experience is equally important. And lest you, the reader, forget that my company is called the Leadership Difference, the behavior of an organization's leaders is paramount to creating a peak performance culture.

WHAT YOU'LL FIND IN THE BOOK

This book shares the metrics that I have discovered while working with thousands of organizations all over the world. My intent is to provide the reader – you – with a guide for organizational development excellence that you can use to evaluate your company's current state, aspire to a desired future state, and construct a strategy for moving from the former to the latter. Each chapter will introduce a key component to peak performance culture, provide a thorough definition of the component including examples and details related to it, and close with some key considerations for you as you evaluate your own situation relative to this metric.

To make the self-assessment of your organizational culture easier, I have included an Peak Performance Culture Assessment. This tool can be used as a discussion starter with an executive team, an interview guide for discussions with a CEO, or a checklist for organizational development implementation. All in all, the process is akin to building a house with a foundation, framework, power sources, and inhabitants.

Few things in life are strictly sequential; the same is true of organizational development. Sure, it would be great if you could read the subsequent chapter, put the book down after completing that chapter, work on that metric, and then return to the book for the next step. Theoretically, if you are planning to begin a business, you might be able to execute on that approach. But the reality is that most readers will be trying to implement improvements during ongoing operations. That means the implementation will be more systemic than sequential. For that reason, I encourage the reader to consume the entire content of the book before assembling a plan for implementing ideas.

All organizations do some things well and other things poorly, just as a house may have good "bones" but poor aesthetics. It is exceptionally rare to find an organization that does everything at the highest level. I certainly haven't found such an organization during my career. Even if your company is succeeding – perhaps *especially* if your company is succeeding – it is important to understand why. That way you don't inadvertently change processes or ideologies that are critical to your success. Even successful organizations can reach an entirely new level of excellence by tightening up a few things.

I encourage you to read each chapter and then pause to reflect on the "key considerations" that are offered at the conclusion. These considerations are not all-inclusive, so feel free to expand on ideas that the content sparked that are unrelated to either the "key considerations" or the Peak Performance Culture Assessment. Once you have documented your thoughts on how the content of that chapter impacts your own organization, you can then move on to the next chapter with a clean slate and clear focus on the next metric. By the time you have completed the book, you will have accumulated an immense number of actionable items that you will need to prioritize and distill into a plan of implementation.

THE PLAN REQUIRES WORK

In my experience, the momentum for organizational improvement is high during the initial parts of the project, but wanes as ideas and opinions give way to the minutia of actionable items. This book has the potential to generate robust and important discussion among executives about the opportunities to improve organizational performance.

The challenge to those responsible for facilitating these discussions and translating them into a meaningful improvement plan will be nudging executives past the big, broad, conceptual discussions and into the exploration of the policies, practices, and experiences that inform the transactions that define operational excellence and peak performance culture. There is no magic pill, mantra, or panacea that will emerge from this book. I wish I could offer that – I could retire. Rather, the value this book offers is a comprehensive template for evaluating the broad subjects that predict success. Beyond that, the hard work falls to you.

If you are working as a team to enhance the performance of your organization, I would recommend tackling each chapter independently, as each chapter could easily be a year-long project. Use the "key considerations" to launch meaningful discussions with the group. This will lead you to identify priorities and tasks that need to be assigned. As I mentioned, no endeavor is strictly sequential, but I have tried to lay out the metrics in a linear perspective. Once you have completed the book, go back to the discussion topics that were generated by each chapter and give serious consideration to them, beginning with those in Chapter 2, then Chapter 3, then 4, and so on. Of course, there are exceptions, but generally this approach should work best.

***

As I read this, I am worried that I have already scared you about the path ahead. My bad. Organizational development is dense and never-ending. But it is also gratifying. Stay focused on small but tangible enhancements and be mindful of making distinctions between activities and impact, lip service versus results. Celebrate each success, no matter how small. That's one of the things that I have noticed over these last 25 years. Peak performance cultures celebrate successes. Often. Be sure to do that.

Most of what you will read in this book are concepts that I learned through various forms of failure – trial and error, solving an existing problem (either in my own company or a client's), researching concepts of which I was ignorant. For that reason, I am most proud of this work. It is real. It is not academic in nature, although I learned some of the content in academic settings. It is practical, applicable, and proven. The ideas work. And they work for multinational companies, nonprofit associations, and the local business. They worked for me and they will work for you.

To address the three questions I posited earlier in this chapter:

- *What is a culture?* In my view, an organization's culture reflects how each team member behaves, executes, prioritizes, and delivers on its expressed vision, strategy, and core ideology as measured by its customers and employees. By this definition, every single organization has a culture. Most exist without intent. They have evolved over time and most do not promote peak performance.

- *What kind of culture drives peak performance?* Those with a clear vision, strategy, and ideology that resonates with the market and generates the results deemed most important by its stakeholders. This requires a rigid commitment to the practices that support these strategies, the creation of exceptional customer and employee experiences, and a passionate leadership approach that is rich with techniques that maximize communication and feed the intrinsic needs of the team. To accomplish such a culture, one needs intent.

- *How do I create a peak performance culture?* Through the hard work and intent described in the chapters that follow. There is no "easy button" for installing a peak performance culture. It requires effort, intent, and the roadmap contained in this book.

Back in 1995, I walked away from a successful corporate career to start my own company with a relatively worthless business plan and no clear understanding of the market for my services. I had a vague notion of my core ideology, but I didn't even know how much money I wanted to make or how to generate a profit and loss statement. Much of this book's content was a complete mystery to me at that time. I would likely have failed but for one attribute on which I built my success until I learned about and implemented the others. Fortunately, I was in possession of one very important attribute for creating a peak performance culture – the foundation. Passion. We'll go into more detail on that in Chapter 1.

Chapter 1 A Foundation of Passion

Passion is joy in action for an enduring period. *Passion* is *joy* in *action* for an *enduring* period. Passion therefore cannot exist without joy, action, and endurance. Passion without joy is work. Passion without action is a dream. Passion without endurance is a phase. True passion must be informed by joy, action, and endurance.

TRUE PASSION IS RARE

Perhaps the biggest challenge in creating a peak performance culture is identifying, cultivating, and continuing passion. There are many threats to operational excellence – toxic leadership, poor strategies, misaligned policies and practices, mediocre customer experiences, less than stellar employee experiences – but none is so prevalent as lack of passion. I am forever struck by the number of people who spend over one-third of their lives engaged in activities (work) from which they derive so little joy.

As Henry David Thoreau said, "The mass of men live lives of quiet desperation."

If you consider that work and sleep combine to consume about two-thirds of our life – and that the preparation and recovering from each will expend another sizable chunk – we have precious little time left over to engage in activity for which we are passionate. It is hard to imagine that doing the laundry, grocery shopping, getting your oil changed, mowing the lawn, and all the other activities most of us spend our "free" time doing will provide an avenue for our passion. Therefore, our vocation offers us the best opportunity for joy over an enduring period. On the other hand, if we are passionate about our work, amazing performance is within our grasp.

If passion fuels individual performance and organizations are simply collectives of individuals, then clearly passion *is* the foundation for any successful organization. It begins with the founder/proprietor/owner/executive/leader, and employees responsible for the organization's performance. I suppose it is possible for an institution to eclipse the passion of its leader, but that shouldn't be necessary. Leaders must drive passion, not limit it. However, sometimes they do the latter. It has been my experience that successful organizations are founded by two types of people. What they have in common is a strong work ethic. They will do what is necessary to will their company to success. However, only one of these types of people will have enduring success—and that is the one who combines this abundant work ethic with a passion for the work being done.

Through the years, I have met many entrepreneurs with amazing ideas that I could not have begun to imagine. I have met brilliant businesspeople with an aptitude for capitalism that I will never possess. I have seen organizations fortunate enough to have immense capital at their disposal or to be located geographically or situationally in such a way that their competition was at an enormous disadvantage. While talent, imagination, money, location, and context are all vital to an organization's success, nothing is more important than passion. Why? Because the dirty secret of success is this: as hard as it is to achieve it, it is infinitely harder to *continue* it. Work ethic—what I think of as desire—is critical to achieving success; but passion is critical for continuing it.

DESIRE VERSUS PASSION

Desire is plentiful in the moment a business begins. The birth of a business is often the result of desire overcoming fear. Starting a business is scary. Risk is high. Rewards are not guaranteed. For a company to exist at all, there was a moment when the desire to create it outweighed the daunting barriers that could – likely would – undermine success. Sure, some businesses begin with ample money and clear advantages. But I'm not talking about those exceptions. I'm talking about the organizations that began with the desire of a single or small group of risk-takers with a vision or, at least, a dream.

These organizations often fail. They fail because running a successful company is hard. Often, the mindset that leads to excellence is also the type of mind that thinks critically; and when you think critically, you continually see problems to solve. While that is an exceptional perspective for continuous improvement, it ensures that you won't relax much, sleep well, or truly ever be completely satisfied. It takes a special quality to propel an individual through the ongoing challenges, setbacks, and uncertainty involved in succeeding. Many start strong, and even achieve success, only to slowly lose their edge (their passion) and watch the organization slide back to mediocrity or worse. Desire most often succumbs to weariness.

There are currently around 150 wineries in the Walla Walla Valley wine region where I live. The Walla Walla Community College's vinicultural and enology program is full of students with dreams of being the next successful winemaker, owner, and/or vineyard manager. Armed with a desire to do the hard work that it takes to succeed in this highly competitive space and the knowledge of how to make wine, they will arrive within a market saturated with competition. To succeed, they work long, arduous days to make, promote, and sell wine. And most will fail.

Desire can get you started. It can even make you successful. But desire is not an infinite vessel of motivation. Desire drains. Desire without joy is not passion.

Family-owned businesses provide an excellent illustration of the difference between desire and passion. There is a belief related to family-owned businesses that the third generation will kill the company. "Shirtsleeves to shirtsleeves in three generations" the saying goes. Working in numerous industries that are populated by family owned businesses, I have seen it firsthand. Generally, the business is founded by a passionate person who works hard, struggles, fights off the adversity, and succeeds using the foundation of passion. They channel their joy into action that endures. The second generation – a daughter or son who has witnessed this epic undertaking – brings fresh ideas, technologies, and, especially, passion to the battle. Often, the company becomes bigger, even more successful, and high performing during this time when both joy and endurance exist to create passion. The second generation saw the original passion and the demands created by the struggle for success. They "caught the bug," as one father explained about his daughter's success with the family business.

Finally, a third generation enters leadership. This individual did not experience or observe the original struggle. They are not aware of how big a role joy played in creating success. While they may have the desire and work ethic necessary to succeed, they don't possess the passion that began and perpetuated the company. They ascend to leadership due to birthright, not because of joy in action. It is not an indictment of the grandchildren's talent or ability, but rather evidence of how necessary passion is when building and sustaining a success.

THE IMPORTANCE OF JOY

I know all about desire. I have displayed it consistently throughout my career. It was desire, roughly synonymous with "possessing a high work ethic," that drove my achievements in the corporate world. It was desire that pushed me to be a television producer for CBS at 22 years old. It was desire that provided the fuel for my journey to the top human resources executive for an international hospitality management company at age 33. But it was also desire that revealed this key revelation to me: desire is not enough to create enduring performance. In fact, desire without passion often results in burnout. It did with me.

I burned out three times. Until I learned the danger of desire without the balance of joy, I continued to succumb to stress. Desire is about effort. Passion is about joy. Effort is finite; joy is self-renewing. My corporate career from 1983 to 1995 was like a twelve-year course on the importance of passion.

By 1995, I had distilled the source of my joy to some very specific activities. I knew I loved educating. Specifically, I loved making people laugh while they learned about themselves, others, and their organization. The things that diverted my attention away from that focus were the things that robbed me of joy, diluted my passion, and resulted in me losing my desire. I feel fortunate to have arrived at this revelation at a relatively young age. As a result, I was able to nudge my career in a direction that better aligned with my passion.

Now, before you start to assume that passion for your vocation makes everything easy – it doesn't. Passion is the foundation for peak performance culture, but it is not the entirety of operational excellence. What passion provides is the building block from which all else can be constructed. It is the perpetual fuel source to deal with all the challenges that will ensue. As an example, after I speak at a large conference, I am often approached by an audience member who says, "I want to do what you do." I take it as it is intended, as a compliment. They see my passion and want to experience what it would be like to feel that way about a job. However, there is a lot more than passion necessary to success. One must have talent, a vision, a strategy, processes, commitment, resiliency, and so on. People see me on the stage. They don't see me in the airport at 4:00 a.m. or writing a proposal on an airplane or doing a conference call in a hotel at 7:00 p.m. They don't imagine the travel schedule, the performance pressure, the revenue generation responsibilities, and all the other tasks – both small and large – that surround the moment of passion. That is why passion is so important to peak performance culture. Without it, no amount of desire can offset the eroding effect of drudgery. But *with* passion, no amount of drudgery is too great to overcome.

You may be asking yourself, "What is my passion?" How does one identify the core values within oneself that can light the fire of joy and keep it lit over time? In my book *The Power of Understanding Yourself*, I explain the metacognitive journey to discover your core ideology, your interactive style preferences, and your values. The clues to your passion certainly lie within the discovery of your purpose and orientation. My core ideology is "to contribute to a loving, happy, and secure family while maintaining my freedom – economically and philosophically – through the facilitation of knowledge and transfer of learning, all for the purpose of being a positive and joyful influence on others." To achieve the level of passion I need to create a high-performing organization and sustain my own personal commitment; my contribution must align with my core ideology. Otherwise, it would bring me no joy. And without joy there can be no passion.

LEADING WITH PASSION

Is your organization led with passion? To achieve peak performance, I believe it should be. To sustain peak performance, I believe it must be.

Passionate leaders are authentic, not superficial. We all know those leaders who *appear* to be passionate. They talk loudly, move fast, bark orders, give moving speeches, and otherwise behave in a manner that would be labeled as "passionate" by an observer. Many times, however, these are simply the manifestations of desire. At worst, they are merely acting the part, trying to coax others to perform when they themselves are not. I find that these behaviors – the overt and exaggerated displays of energy and enthusiasm—are rarely exhibited by truly passionate leaders.

Passionate leaders are engaged. They attend meetings, not to share directives but to understand the details of the organization's current state. They listen to those who work in the trenches, where the organization touches their clients. They understand that while they may have authority, it is the team members that have impact. They get excited about successes and take failures personally. They are compassionate – exhibiting as much concern for the welfare of their employees as they do their biggest customers. They care. While they may never be completely satisfied with the organizational performance – because passionate people are driven—they always take time to understand the people around them and inspire them in the way *they* need to be inspired. They appreciate, empower, develop, and relate. They experience joy at work, and that is critical. They work hard and have found a way to manage the stress and time demands associated with being an engaged leader—because passion, with its endless supply of joy, armors them against duress.

Even great leaders burn out if they don't have enough joy in their life. Ultimately, that is the distinction between desire and passion. Leading by desire is burning a finite fuel source. Leading by passion is perpetual.

As we examine the five metrics of peak performance cultures in the chapters that follow, one thing will become abundantly clear: building a peak performance culture is hard. I often joke with my clients as I introduce each metric by saying, "This sounds hard, right? Well, it is. But it's easier than the next one." It only gets a nervous laugh.

Great organizations don't exist without a foundation of passion. At least, they don't exist long. And passion without joy is just desire that is impossible to maintain without burnout. I know. As I shared earlier in this chapter, I burned out three times in traditional careers before I started the Leadership Difference, Inc. I thought I was passionate about radio and television when I started in broadcasting, but I was done less than five years later. Same with retail and hospitality. Each time I rose quickly up the organizational chart based on high amounts of desire only to find myself exhausted, resentful, and unhappy. It wasn't until I understood my core ideology that I was able to tap into the well of joy necessary to sustain passion for an enduring period.

If you are responsible for an organization, department, team, or even just your own personal contribution to an organization, ask yourself this simple question: "Does my job give me joy?" If it does, then you have a shot at sustaining the passion necessary for the foundation of peak performance. If it does not, I would recommend taking inventory of your core ideology and finding a way to do *that* for a living. Heck, maybe you should pick up a copy of *The Power of Understanding Yourself*. I narrate the audible book version. <Wink>

Key Considerations

- Passion in leadership is the basis for all peak performance cultures.
- Passion is joy in action for an enduring period.
- Desire, which is roughly the same as possessing a great work ethic, can propel peak performance for a finite period, but it is ultimately a limited fuel source. Passion is an unlimited fuel source.
- Creating a peak performance culture is hard and will require an unlimited fuel source for personal peak performance.
- Understanding your own core ideology is critical for identifying your passion.

Chapter 2 Horizontal Alignment

My presumption is that all business owners began their business with two things: the passion (or, perhaps, simply desire) that I discussed in the last chapter, *and* a sincere belief that their concept would be successful. The odd "I needed a tax write-off" scenario aside, I am confident that everyone who starts a business believes that they have a product or service that will resonate with the market and make them money. The good news is that the easiest of all five metrics is testing this belief by creating horizontal alignment. The less good news is that horizontal alignment – while easier than the other four metrics of peak performance cultures – is still very challenging. The *truly* bad news is that few organizations effectively accomplish even this metric and, worse yet, few even try. Thankfully, since you picked up a copy of this book, you are the exception!

Horizontal alignment, combined with vertical alignment (discussed in the next chapter), forms the organization's framework. It is the fundamental knowledge of three things: what's happening in the market, what are the measures of our success, and what is our plan for linking those two (Figure 2.1). Achieving alignment means ensuring that your business plan

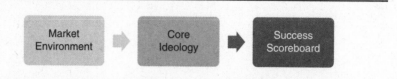

FIGURE 2.1   The basics of horizontal alignment.

responds to the market in which your business exists in such a way as to generate the desired measurements on your success scoreboard. I approach horizontal alignment in a sort of nonlinear, reverse engineering way. To borrow from Stephen Covey, I begin with the end in mind. Since the end of horizontal alignment is our success scoreboard, let's start there.

SUCCESS SCOREBOARD

How will you know if your organization is successful? Fundamentally, you will want to use three quantitative measures to determine success: profitability (or fiscal solvency for a nonprofit organization), efficiency, and stakeholder satisfaction/retention. Nonprofits and not-for-profit organizations must still achieve successful fiscal measures; in fact, the financial achievements may be even more important to them. To keep things simple, I will use a traditional for-profit organization as the model, but the same concepts are true for other forms of entities.

First Measure: Profit

The exact amount of the profit goal is an executive decision and based on the financial needs and aspirations of ownership. Suffice it to say, it is a very rare organization that is *not* expected to turn a profit. So, for the purposes of this explanation, let's just use "profit" as a synonym for the money that ownership requires the organization to generate on the bottom line of a profit and loss statement. Achieving that figure is one of the success scoreboard measures. Interestingly, achieving the target or even exceeding it can be a double-edged sword for a business. Too often, profit is weighted disproportionately heavily relative to the other components of success. There are many unhealthy organizations with exceptional profit performance. This tendency can be devastating to the organization as they often overlook the following critical measures because of an abundance of profit. Doing so can result in significant damage as markets evolve.

Second Measure: Efficiency

From 2003 to 2007, a significant amount of my business revenues was generated through clients who were both directly and indirectly impacted by the mortgage boon. I worked with mortgage bankers, mortgage insurers, home builders, professional associations for lending, banking and building industries, home remodelers, luxury appliance manufacturers, and designers. I spoke at many realtor associations to packed crowds populated by relatively new real estate professionals who had tripled their incomes in a couple of years by transitioning into this vocation. Everywhere I went, money was plentiful, and profitability was at record levels. There was only one problem. These incredible profits were concealing a toxic and terminal organizational threat: inefficiency. It was the business equivalent of "fat and happy." More accurately, many organizations and individuals had become fat and sloppy.

I remember being struck by how many leaders – respected, long-term professionals in the field – would come up to me after a presentation and share with me how worried they were about the sustainability of this market situation. They seemed keenly aware that the environment was changing and that when the "chickens came home to roost" the entire industry would suffer significantly. Yet few made changes in their operation. I remember only a handful of clients who made wholesale adjustments in their business strategy in anticipation of more turbulent times. Most others were content to ride the hot hand.

I was appreciative of the siren calls of those professionals as it inspired me to pivot toward the pharmaceutical and insurance industries, but not without sustaining my own wounds.

When the mortgage boon abruptly ended in 2008, many of the same organizations and individuals who had experienced the apparent phenomenal success the preceding several years were now thrust into a precipitous decline in profitability. In fact, many became unprofitable, and more than a few companies and people were driven from the industry entirely. That's because in their rush to make more and more money, they failed to create the efficient processes and infrastructure necessary to protect against market fluctuations. When the market suddenly declined, they didn't just see their profits shrink; they saw them disappear. My own small firm took a hit. While we were able to survive, I can still remember those hard lessons. They showed very clearly how operational inefficiency can be deadly.

The success scoreboard must contain measures of both profitability and efficiency. Efficiency will not wholly protect an organization from severe market fluctuations, but it does allow companies to remain profitable during the natural ebbs and flows. Efficiency also shows discipline, in that companies that maintain diligence and stay committed to operational best practices even as they achieve profitability goals are well positioned to endure whatever the market environment may throw at them.

Of course, not all market developments can be foreseen. The best insurance against unforeseen threats to organizational success is efficiency. While market is a leading driver for profits, leadership is a leading driver for efficiency. Unfortunately, too many leaders allow the market to drive both.

Third Measure: Stakeholder Satisfaction and Retention

The third measure on the success scoreboard is more complicated – stakeholder satisfaction and retention. Stakeholder satisfaction is a behavioral metric. Since organizations are simply a collective of people unified around a common business strategy providing services to other people (individually, business to consumer, or collectively, business to business), one can anticipate that the behavior of the people involved is of critical importance to the company. The success scoreboard must measure the relative satisfaction of three sets of people with three distinct perspectives: owners, customers, and employees. Further, one must be mindful that a fundamental tenet of human behavior is that behavior breeds behavior (more on that in a later chapter). This means that any dissatisfaction within one of these three populations will inevitably lead to dissatisfaction in another.

It is this last sentence that is so important. Keeping owners happy is a pretty obvious metric for organizational success. I can honestly tell you that in my 30-plus years of working inside companies and outside as a consultant/speaker, I have *never* discovered an organization that survives ownership dissatisfaction. Heck, many organizations don't survive *satisfied* owners! Owners are also the most likely of this triarchy to voice dissatisfaction assertively for the purposes of changing the operation. In that regard, their feedback is the most accessible of the three, and while I have known more than a few irrational owners, it is still the easiest feedback to define.

Over the last 40 years or so, the rise of customer centricity has created a broadly accepted view that customer satisfaction is critical to organizational success. Virtually every industry in a capitalistic economic structure faces competitive forces for their products and services. As a result, customers who are not happy with their current service provider can pursue other options. Even those companies who enter markets as the sole service provider will have only a short advantage before competitors show up. The Walla Walla Valley wine industry is a great example. It essentially began when Leonetti Cellars, founded in 1977, produced a wine that would be named the best Cabernet Sauvignon in the nation by *Wine & Spirits* magazine. At the time, much of the world responded with, "Who is Leonetti Cellars, and where is Walla Walla, Washington?" Today, over 150 wineries exist in this market. Success generates competition. Thus, satisfying your customer is a no-brainer. However, customer satisfaction does not assure customer *retention*.

Importance of Customer Satisfaction

Satisfaction is a complicated concept. Recently, I was speaking at an event in Miami and the client had arranged for a car/driver to pick me up at the airport and take me to my hotel. I arrived on time in Miami and promptly received a text from my driver directing me to meet him in baggage claim. There, I spied my driver displaying a sign with my name on it. The two of us then walked to his car, got in, and he drove me to my hotel. One hour later, I received an email from the transportation company asking for feedback.

- Was the driver on time to pick you up?
- Was the driver professional?
- Was the car clean?
- Did you arrive at your intended destination?
- Did you arrive at your destination on time?

These were all legitimate questions and represent the fundamentals of measuring my satisfaction. I answered "yes" to all five. But here's the thing. I would expect *any* transportation experience to fulfill these expectations. Yes, I was satisfied; but that didn't mean I was now a lifelong customer of this company. While satisfaction is important, it is retention that measures success.

When we measure customer satisfaction, it is imperative that we are measuring those things that ensure loyalty to our business and not merely those that reflect that we have fulfilled the fundamental requirements of the marketplace. Had any of my answers to the survey questions asked by the transportation company been "no," I certainly would not have used them again. However, simply navigating a transaction within the general expectations of any customer doesn't *wow* me – or anyone else. Success with customers means you are delivering a product or service that is compelling enough to ensure that your customers won't leave you for the competition. Additionally, by providing services that exceed the customer's fundamental expectations, you can charge more for them. This is called "value-added" service.

Value-added service allows you to charge more while still winning loyalty. It can also be used as a differentiator for your customers when pricing is equal to your competitors. Identifying the additional elements of a customer experience that have value to your customer and delivering them better than your competitors is an excellent retention strategy. Even better is to find those value-added experiences that cost very little to provide but that the customer views as extremely valuable. These services will improve both retention and profitability.

One of my favorite value-added experiences was provided by Rosen Shingle Creek Resort and Spa in Orlando, Florida. I facilitated a leadership development series for Harris Rosen's hotels for twenty years. Almost every month during those two decades, I would stay at one of his properties. The staff knew me, and I knew them. Arriving at the hotel was like visiting family. All of this is value-added service, of course, but the moment that blew me away was a tiny little thing. Upon arriving at Rosen Shingle Creek in the middle of a particularly challenging travel stretch, I checked in and headed to my guest room. There, in front of the door to my room, was a special mat that simply said, "Welcome Back." There were no other mats in front of any room. It was meant just for me – a frequent guest who was returning yet again. Other than the cost of the mat, which I assume would be used many times for similar circumstances, this gesture didn't cost much at all. Yet the impact on me was tremendous. That is value-added service.

The Need for Customer Retention

The wine industry is a great example of the dangers of focusing on customer satisfaction instead of customer retention. In each of the 150 or so tasting rooms around Walla Walla, customers are sampling wine served by an associate of the winery. Minimally, the patrons expect a pleasant interaction, information about the wine that matches their need for details, and a comfortable spot to enjoy the samplings. Any winery that fails to provide that will leave their customers unsatisfied. Satisfied or not, the customer will likely pay a tasting fee for the experience. The unsatisfied customer will not buy any wine, however. Worse, they will likely share their unsatisfying experience with other customers, which can damage the brand more broadly. The satisfied customer may or may not buy wine, but they are unlikely to hurt your reputation.

The true measure of success in a tasting room is signing up a customer to be part of their wine club. This assures 2–4 wine shipments (sales!) each year of larger transaction amounts than a typical tasting room purchase. Club members join because they experienced something of value that exceeded their fundamental expectations. As a result, they are willing to continue the relationship going forward. That's customer retention.

So, if you were constructing a success scoreboard for a winery, it is more important to measure club membership than customer satisfaction. If the latter is high and the former is low, you are not horizontally aligned with the marketplace in such a way as to be successful long term. If club membership is high, it is almost assured that customer satisfaction is also high – meaning you are horizontally aligned. I know, it's a little confusing. Peak performance culture isn't easy.

Think of it in sports terms. An organization that satisfies customers but doesn't retain them is equivalent to a baseball team that plays .500 ball – wins and losses are even. This team is doing okay, but they aren't going to win a championship. An organization that retains customers is playing at a championship level.

Consider one last point on the importance of focusing on customer retention rather than customer satisfaction. The cost in time, resources, and money to *acquire* a customer is very high. Entire marketing budgets are applied to this pursuit.

The process of enticing a customer into your business to experience your products and services is both involved and expensive. Once they have entered your orbit, being able to capture them for future opportunities spreads that initial cost over several transactions – in effect, lowering that initial marketing cost. If the customer does not return after one or two transactions, that cost of acquisition skyrockets. To make matters worse, you now must spend money to find another customer to replace the one you just lost.

All of this is to say that your customer satisfaction measurements are likely fool's gold. What you want to know is more specific:

- Why do you choose to be our customer?
- What makes us special compared to our competitors?
- How can we continue to improve those things to ensure you continue to be our customer?
- What else can we do to deserve your business?

If you know the answers to those four questions, you will be successful.

One of the most innovative techniques for continually monitoring the answers is the Client Advisory Board (CAB). I have assisted a few organizations with this process, and I wish it was more common. The CAB is a collection of representatives from influential customers. Optimally, you want the board populated by the individuals who have the most impact over the decision to utilize your company versus your competitors. At regular intervals (I like quarterly), this group of 8–12 members meets to discuss current issues and recommendations. They are great barometers for changes in the market environment and can provide useful business intel that can allow your company to anticipate and respond to industry trends. They can also help troubleshoot service deficiencies and identify value-added services to enhance market differentiation. Finally, membership on a client advisory board reinforces retention of your key customers. We will explore the concept of client advisory boards as well as client awareness councils in Chapter 5 when we dive deeper into the customer experience.

Employees as Stakeholders

Employees are the one stakeholder group whose satisfaction has been less attended to historically. Just like with customers, retention is critical and supersedes mere satisfaction when measuring success. A study by *Employee Benefit News* found that the organization's cost of losing an employee was 33 percent of their annual salary. Stated differently, losing a full-time employee costs nearly 700 times their hourly rate. Incredible!

Most organizations give lip service to their commitment to employee satisfaction but far fewer apply measurement tools to monitor it. Those that do monitor employee satisfaction often fall into the same trap as customer satisfaction surveys. They measure maintenance rather than retention issues. The employee may be entirely satisfied with their job but leave it for another that pays just a little bit more or is a little more convenient or offers more opportunities. Just like the customer who is satisfied but not loyal, employees can be happy but still looking. Losing either is expensive.

Employee turnover is an obvious marker for employee satisfaction. Low turnover relative to the industry can be an excellent way to determine success. However, it is important to understand why people are leaving the organization. Some industries are prone to higher turnover than others. The market can impact employee turnover, too. If your new hire pool is composed of college students, for example, you can expect higher turnover. So, turnover alone is not a perfect measure of employee satisfaction. As much as possible, conduct exit interviews with any employee leaving. This can be an excellent source of information regarding pockets of toxicity within your culture and provide clues to enhancing the employee experience (more on that in a later chapter). You may also find out that people are leaving for a little more money. This is reflective of a culture in which employees are satisfied but not loyal – where a small wage increase will lure them away.

Later in this book, I examine several elements of a corporate culture that can elevate employee satisfaction to loyalty and increase retention (see Chapter 4, "Leadership Ideology"). I'll also outline five human resources systems that can generate more employee retention when well executed (see Chapter 6, "The Employee Experience"). For horizontal alignment purposes, employee satisfaction/retention – just like customer satisfaction/retention – must be consistently measured, monitored, and used to drive strategy. Since behavior breeds behavior and since the most vulnerable population of stakeholders are employees, an organization that fails to satisfy and retain their own team members effectively will soon experience declines in customer retention and ownership satisfaction.

MARKET ENVIRONMENT

I like to think of the success scoreboard as an output of the organization. If we are effectively horizontally aligned, the product of our efforts is the achievement of the success measures. To accomplish this output, we must effectively navigate the input – the market environment. This includes a vast number of considerations, ranging from client expectations, demographics, and competitive pressures, to legislative environments, market conditions, local economics, tax and zoning details, and many more. Each industry will have its own considerations. Detailed and comprehensive market intelligence allows leadership to generate the most effective organizational plan to achieve the success scoreboard. Furthermore, the organization must continually monitor the market environment to identify emerging trends that will impact their effectiveness.

Consider the market conditions in homebuilding that I discussed in the success scoreboard section. Many of the executives with whom I worked before the market downturn would share their concerns about the potential volatility years before 2007. Unfortunately, few of them preemptively adjusted their horizontal alignment to account for this change. Successful horizontal alignment not only involves connecting the current market environment to your success scoreboard; it also requires that you make the necessary changes when market conditions, emerging technology, or consumer tastes evolve.

In my adopted hometown of Walla Walla, there are those roughly 150 wineries – in a town that has less than 50,000 people in the area, is three-plus hours away from a large metropolitan area, and has a small regional airport with flights to one city (Seattle) three times a day. Each year, many new enology and viniculture professionals graduate from the local community college with dreams of entering this crowded market. They join more than a handful of retired professionals and existing wineries from other wine regions with the same desire. In the five years that my lovely bride and I have lived here, we have seen dozens of wineries enter the market and dozens more fade away. The winery market in Walla Walla is as volatile as it is attractive.

I have rarely had a bad glass of wine from the local wineries. Walla Walla Valley is a truly magical place with many fantastic vineyards. Finding quality grapes is easy; in fact, there is a far greater supply of juice than there is a demand for it. This creates a wonderful opportunity for local winemakers who cannot afford to create estate wines – wines made from grapes grown in vineyards owned by the winery. Winemakers can gain access to quality grapes, perform the winemaking process through shared winemaking facilities to reduce their capital investment in equipment, and sell their wines at tasting rooms that can be procured at reasonable rental rates at various locations around the city. Entry into the industry is affordable, the business sounds attractive and – with a couple of years of training – is rather easy to learn. There remains, however, one daunting barrier to success. Well, not one, but 150: the competition.

There are many legal issues to address when starting a winery. Let's assume a potential new winery has sufficient expertise in winemaking, a supply of quality grapes, access to winemaking equipment, and an accessible, appealing wine tasting room experience. Let's imagine they have also successfully navigated local, state, and federal regulations. There still remains that huge hurdle to success. Why would a consumer buy my wine over those offered by my 150 competitors? Based on my experiences as a professional in the wine field (I am an advanced wine sommelier, provide training and consulting to the wine industry, work at a local winery's tasting room that my lovely bride manages, and am a frequent consumer), I can tell you that most of these wineries have not asked themselves that question: *Why me?* Many succeed or fail based on the location of their tasting room, their positive reviews in the wine press, or their heritage/reputation within the industry. Even more appear to have no specific core ideology designed to react to this competitive market environment and generate the success scoreboard to which they aspire.

Core ideology is the link between the input of market environment and output of success scoreboard and the key to horizontal alignment. Simply put, core ideology answers three questions:

- **Who** do we want to be (vision)?
- **Why** would a customer choose us over our competitors (mission)?
- **How** do we achieve the *who* and *why* (strategy)?

WHY ME? THE CORE IDEOLOGY

We think of a company as an organization that provides products and/or services to the public in exchange for a fee. An organization is a collection of individuals with a shared purpose – presumably to provide value (in the way of products and/or services) to a market. The definition of both almost always focuses on the belief that these collectives (companies and organizations) are product and/or service based. When you ask someone what their company does, they answer by describing the products and/or services.

Peak performance organizations define themselves differently. Sure, they recognize that they must provide a product/service that the market desires. The problem is, so do all their competitors. What will differentiate them is their core ideology.

Makeup of a Core Ideology

Core ideologies are a combination of vision, mission, and strategy. Vision is the desired future state for the organization. It is a clearly articulated description of what the organization will look like when they have achieved their goals. Once achieved, the organization can aspire to a new, enhanced vision or strive to maintain what they believe is a model for excellence. Visions may or may not be shared with customers, but they are vitally important in determining the organization's direction and monitoring the ongoing alignment between the market environment and the success scoreboard.

Some visions are detailed, addressing exactly what the desired future state will look like. Others are more conceptual and aspirational, serving as a continuous point of comparison to keep the organization tethered to a core ideology. For example, my company – the Leadership Difference, Inc. – has a vision: "To positively affect the life of every person with whom we come in contact." This statement guides all our activities and provides the basis for comparison to ensure our mission and strategy are consistent with our vision.

Mission is the vehicle that will take us to that state. Think of mission as your "special sauce." It is the one thing you believe you can do better than your competitors. A mission is what you base your brand on, and how you will promote your company. Think about how some of the iconic auto insurance companies promote their mission with brand slogans. "You're in good hands with Allstate" articulates their belief that policyholders will be well taken care of when they have a claim. "Like a good neighbor, State Farm is there" indicates that the policyholder can rely on them to be there when they need help. "We know a thing or two because we've seen a thing or two" (Farmers Insurance) indicates that this organization has the experience and expertise to handle anything that the policyholder may experience. My mission is "To provide thought-provoking perspectives on work and life shared through humor." Consequently, our brand slogan is "Laugh and learn!" My core ideology then states that we will have a positive impact on you by providing laughter and education.

Strategy is the route we plan to take when applying our mission to achieve our vision. If vision is "Who are we?" and mission is "Why are we?" then strategy is "How are we?" It is arguably the most challenging element of core ideology in that it requires the examination of pathways to propel the organization from the current state to the desired future state. There are a lot of moving parts within an organization and it is very easy to get bogged down in the details. Having facilitated many strategic planning retreats, I can attest to the dangers of wasting entire days – even weeks – on discussions about very specific operational elements when examining ways to improve the organization. In the next chapter we will explore "vertical alignment." Many of the issues that distract from a good strategic planning session are components of vertical alignment (initiatives and action items), not horizontal alignment (strategy).

These strategies are mostly broad, like the concept of customer centricity. Customer centricity is a strategy that elevates the client's perspective into every decision made by the organization. Slightly different than "the customer is always right" – which sounds more like a brand slogan emerging from a mission – customer centricity challenges the organization to evaluate the impact of all decisions on the client's experience. As such, it demands that the customer is always top of mind. That sounds like an obvious strategy, but most companies are not customer centric. In fact, most of the companies that claim to be customer centric are not. One of my clients, Stu Needleman – a C-suite-level executive in the pharmaceutical industry who is an evangelist for a customer centric strategy – often starts a meeting by asking, "Who here is in sales?" Anyone who doesn't raise their hand gets a lecture on customer centricity.

For customer centricity to be a strategy, each member of the organization must manifest the client's perspective when making decisions, providing services, or selling. That is how a strategy works. At the Leadership Difference, Inc., we use a variation of a customer centricity strategy called a consultative approach. We spend time understanding the client's needs, identify the most important ones, and recommend services that target those needs – even if the client has expressed an interest in alternative services. A consultative approach elevates the organization's expertise to the same level as the client's needs. That is a strategy.

Perhaps it goes without saying, but a successful core ideology is one that resonates with the market environment and produces the desired results as identified in the success scoreboard. That is horizontal alignment. The beautiful part of this is that it is not one size fits all. Within any market, many core ideologies can exist. The key is to have a vision, mission, and strategy that will excite the environment.

Comparing Two Wineries' Core Ideologies

Back to Walla Walla's wine industry. For a new winery to succeed, they must offer more than being simply another option for the consumer. An eye-catching label or creative name is not a strategy. They must identify and articulate the mission they will deliver on to achieve their vision of success. How does an organization know if they have a core ideology? They stick out. They can tell their story in a couple of sentences. Core ideology is to an organization what an elevator pitch is to a salesperson.

Consider Cayuse Winery. Cayuse is a legend in Walla Walla and the envy of savvy, serious wine collectors around the world. If you are only a casual wine drinker, chances are you have never heard of Cayuse. Even if you are a full-fledged wine enthusiast, it is quite likely you have never consumed a Cayuse wine and probably never will. Why? Because they are impossible to get. That seems like a very odd core ideology for a for-profit winery, but that is exactly what makes Cayuse special. Cayuse Winery began as a contrarian venture, so the fact that they continue their success using an unconventional core ideology is not a surprise.

Cayuse was founded in 1997 when Christophe Baron purchased some land notable for the large stones that littered it. While the locals viewed the stones as an unappealing and challenging barrier to work with (breaking equipment and adding unnecessary expenses to vineyard management), Christophe saw a terroir (aspect of land and soil composition) that matched the famed Southern Rhone wine appellation in France called Châteauneuf-du-Pape. Nothing in the Washington wine region could compare with the prestige of Châteauneuf-du-Pape – at least, not until Christophe planted Cayuse.

His vision was to produce a wine to rival those from France. He produced mainly Syrahs, Syrahs that did not taste like the other Washington Syrahs. Like the vineyard from which they come, they are earthy, minerally, and big. If you could make wine out of a rock, it would taste like Cayuse. That is a compliment; wine is made better when it comes from vines that struggle. They beg for food, elevating any meal in which that wine is included, and can bottle-age for decades. That is the vision of Cayuse: to create an iconic Old World Syrah in Washington. Christophe's mission is to craft food-friendly wines of incredible depth, individuality, and character – all from fruit grown entirely using biodynamic farming methods. The wine press fell in love and wine connoisseurs came in droves. Demand grew. And grew.

Most companies, when faced with growing demand, increase supply. That's generally a no-brainer strategy. But not Cayuse.

They embraced a strategy of exclusivity. Here's the actual language on their website under the "Contact Us" tab: "Thank you for your interest in Cayuse Vineyards. Due to the demands in the vineyards and wine studio, we regret that we are not able to offer tours or tastings. Please don't hesitate to contact us with other requests. Thanks." I mean, if I can't taste the wine, what "other requests" would I have at a winery – am I right?

They sell all their wine to restaurants, distributors, and Cayuse club members. There is a long waiting list to be added to the club. They have a wine tasting room in downtown Walla Walla that is open *one day each year*. On that day, Cayuse club members can come and pick up their allotted wines. It is so popular that the entire town of Walla Walla and the 150 other wineries celebrate that day with Cayuse Weekend. There are special events at other wineries, restaurants, hotels, and retail shops. Imagine a company whose products are in such a demand that their *competitors celebrate* the moment they make them available to their customers. I giggle at the thought of Microsoft celebrating the new iPhone release, or Chevrolet throwing a party to recognize the arrival of the new Ford Mustang. That is an amazing strategy to complete a well-honed core ideology. It's essentially, "We are amazing, and you can't have it." Brilliant.

A few miles away from the exclusive Cayuse estate (not open to the public, of course) is Sleight of Hand Cellars. Sleight of Hand's core ideology is very different than that of Cayuse. While Cayuse makes it nearly impossible to get their wine –a strategy that has become a significant part of their core ideology – Sleight of Hand's expressed mission is "serious wines without serious attitudes."

Founded ten years after Cayuse by Trey Busch and Jerry and Sandy Solomon, there is a rock and roll vibe in their Walla Walla tasting room. Visitors can select the vinyl record they want to provide the soundtrack for their tasting experience. As they have increased in popularity, they have increased their production and opened an additional tasting room in Seattle. Their club shipments include free downloads of songs from the famous record label Sub Pop. "Great wine, great music and lots of fun – that's our recipe for the Sleight of Hand lifestyle," is the stated core ideology, with the "lots of fun" representing their strategy.

While the core ideologies couldn't be more different, both Cayuse and Sleight of Hand benefit by having a clear, articulated core ideology. It is no surprise that they are two of the most successful wineries in Walla Walla – distinguishing themselves from the crowded field of competitors by horizontally aligning the market environment with a core ideology that generates the success scoreboard. They are also evidence that there are many paths to success, as long as you are horizontally aligned.

HOW DO YOU IDENTIFY YOUR CORE IDEOLOGY?

For some organizations, particularly small ones like mine, the core ideology is largely an extension of a personal belief system. I am passionate about education and like to make people laugh. Consequently, "Laugh and Learn" was a pretty easy brand slogan to promote. The mission of "positively affecting the life of each person we meet" was essentially taken from my personal mission statement that includes "being a positive and joyful influence on others."

By executing on a professional core ideology that aligns with your personal joy, you can generate the passion necessary to maintain peak performance. Of course, this core ideology still must respond to the market environment and generate successful results. If what makes you passionate doesn't resonate with the market or produce success – well, let's just say that nothing is worse than doing something well that need not be done at all. All apologies to Peter Drucker for the paraphrasing.

Larger organizations are different. Predictably, it is far more challenging to both identify and execute on a core ideology when you are involving 50, 500, or 5,000 people. In these cases, identifying a core ideology has less to do with a single person's beliefs and more to do with the capabilities of the group and the needs and desires of the marketplace. That's why so many organizations have underwhelming, inaccurate, or no core ideology at all. Those who endeavor to identify a core ideology generally do so by sequestering leadership in a room for a spirited discussion that lasts about 48 hours. The results of these retreats are often mixed and depend largely on the commitment of those involved to identify a worthwhile final product – as well as their efforts to drive it through the organization via vertical alignment (covered in the next chapter). Oh, and these retreats often include golf and booze, so priorities can shift suddenly.

That's not to say that companies don't successfully create effective core ideologies. The examples of Cayuse and Sleight of Hand are good ones. Many of my clients, large and small, have developed them. When I am asked to facilitate these exercises, I utilize a few tools that have enhanced the likelihood of a successful outcome.

Spend Some Time Evaluating the Leadership Team's Culture

The goal here is to move the participating executives responsible for the core ideology from individual contributor to team member as early as possible. One of the challenges I have noticed in doing leadership development for organizations is that the individual leaders are often more comfortable with their functional responsibilities than their role as an organization leader. They often have nearly complete autonomy within their department, which frequently means they lead with an autocratic or directive style. Within the organization working with their fellow functional leaders (peers) on companywide strategies, they must arrive at consensus or at least be inclusive in decision-making efforts. Doing a team building exercise early on can shift their perspective from function to group and begin the process of identifying the leadership team's culture.

I utilize the content from my book *The Power of Understanding People*, which includes a self-assessment to identify which of twelve Hollywood movie characters you most communicate like. It is a fun way to better appreciate the diverse ways with which each member of the leadership team communicates and can provide insight into the team's preferences, strengths, and vulnerabilities.

For example, if all or nearly all the executives share the same interactive style, this indicates a strong preference (culture) for a certain way of thinking and communicating. This "lean" will generate obvious strengths and vulnerabilities. It also often makes consensus easier to achieve but risks significant blind spots when crafting the strategy due to their singular perspective. Conversely, teams that have diverse styles may struggle to reach agreements on strategic decisions but arrive at much more comprehensive and thoughtful ones when they do. Of course, they may also self-destruct in the process. Both compositions have strengths and weaknesses, and knowing these predispositions before beginning strategic planning can be very useful to the process.

As a participant in the corporate world, I was also impressed by the effectiveness of experiential exercises in creating a foundation of cohesiveness and unity. My favorite version of this approach was the ropes course, which introduces the team to a series of challenges that are both mental and physical in nature. Ropes courses can be designed to accommodate the level of physicality appropriate for the team. I have found that some people experience a true epiphany when confronted with a physical challenge that serves as a metaphor for a professional situation. When my clients get stuck, I often drag out three tennis balls and a stopwatch and introduce them to the "ball industry." I won't give it away here because you may be a participant someday. Suffice it to say, watching a dozen executives flinging tennis balls around a room for an hour can create some creative energy and unification of perspective. There are several other ways to make the leadership team more cohesive and learn about their behaviors as a unit. Escape rooms, charitable activities, scavenger hunts, cooking classes, and so on can all be constructed as team building events.

There are some foundational behaviors that are necessary for a leadership team to manifest to successfully arrive at a core ideology. These sound a lot like those corporate values that are promoted on almost every company website under "About Us." As you'll discover in a future chapter, I am a bit skeptical of those corporate values. However, a few are important to team function. I think of them more as the foundation of a high-performing leadership culture. Here are the ones that I find to be most valuable:

Trust

Constructing a useful core ideology requires some tough talk about the organizational current state. It is imperative that each member of the leadership team be able to talk openly and honestly about their perspective without fear of damaging relationships or facing consequences. The leadership team must operate with the knowledge that their ideas and feedback will be evaluated without acrimony or long-term consequences. Each member of a leadership team should feel comfortable providing constructive feedback to their peers without fear of reprisal.

Engagement

Engagement, for me, is a combination of interest, input, and enthusiasm. Engaged teams display an excitement about the process and are eager to contribute. The best strategic planning facilitation sessions in which I participated required little of me except the occasional redirection when discussions got off on a tangent or drifted into details better left for the implementation stage.

There is nothing more frustrating to me than facilitating a discussion about an organization's core ideology with a leadership team and observing a participant's (or an entire team's) disinterest. This is most common when dealing with an organization's board of directors and is often reflective of a poorly selected board member. Boards populated by apathetic members damage the organization. A lack of engagement can happen at the executive team level as well. To me, this is symptomatic of a very unhealthy company. If executive leadership doesn't care about core ideology, there is no hope that the rest of the organization will.

Idea Generation

Having a robust, spirited conversation about a variety of options is the hallmark of a healthy leadership team. This means that all members are heard, and all ideas considered. Any behavior or mechanism that serves to limit ideas is working contrary to creating an effective core ideology.

I learned of the expectations that the YMCA of the USA had for their board of directors while providing leadership development for a local center. They viewed board governance as the fulfillment of three responsibilities: fiduciary (fiscal monitoring), strategic, and generative. I like that clarity. Whether it's a board of directors or executive leadership team, I have found that they all understand their role in the first two: fiduciary and strategic. Generative is more uncommon. Generative involves the responsibility to identify changes in the market environment in advance of their impact on the success scoreboard. This allows for changes to core ideology that anticipate these changes rather than react to them. After all, the surfer starts paddling before the wave arrives, lest he be wiped off his board.

Collaboration

The whole should be better than the sum of the parts. Leadership teams are composed of functional leaders, or executives from other organizations in the case of boards of directors, who are likely very successful. This can create some ego issues that potentially interfere with collaboration. Effective leadership teams can set aside their personal needs and perspectives to work together to create a core ideology. This is more evidence for the value of doing team building functions for boards and executive leadership teams.

Clear Expectations

Knowing exactly what is expected in terms of behavior, time-lines, deliverables, and the like allows each team member to contribute in a consistent and appropriate manner. Setting aside time specifically for the development of a core ideology and identifying the desired outcomes for the process is essential to success.

***

To help you assess the current state of your leadership team (or board), at the end of this chapter I have included two Peak Performance Leadership Assessments: one for nonprofit boards and one for executive leadership teams. High-performing leadership teams/boards typically achieve a cumulative score of 12 or higher on each cluster. One final note, when I administer this form to teams/boards, I use a version that does not include the five characteristics (the cluster totals that follow each of the five sets of questions).

Spend Time Thinking About the Market Environment

I find it very useful for the group to discuss three things:

- What does the market expect from an organization in our industry?
- What do our competitors do well?
- Are there products/services that do not currently exist that would meet the needs of the marketplace or create a new desire?

These three questions will generate discussion related to the market environment. It can be quite telling about the current state of the organization if the group struggles to answer these. In a perfect world, the leadership team should be able to answer at least the first two easily and thoroughly. If they cannot, or if there is a difference of opinion, there is a clear lack of market intelligence that needs to be addressed. Assembling a successful core ideology will require that leadership knows what the market expects, who is currently delivering that, and if there exist some gaps not being served by the market.

Spend Time Honestly Evaluating Your Current State

This is the part of the process that I call "Naked and Afraid." If an organization is going to develop a clear strategy as part of their core ideology, they must begin from an honest current state. To do otherwise would be like getting directions to a destination on Google Maps from a location that you are not currently at. The directions may be accurate, but they are not useful.

I still find the good, old-fashioned SWOT analysis to be the best tool for generating the organization's current state. For those not familiar with this iconic resource, it challenges participants to list the Strengths, Weaknesses, Opportunities, and Threats that currently exist within the organization. This activity can be long and arduous, but the more comprehensive the SWOT analysis, the more accurate the organizational current state becomes. It is completely okay – encouraged, really – for the leadership team to be critical of the current state of the organization. That's healthy and a hallmark of peak performance.

Recently, I was facilitating a strategic planning session with a local chapter of a chamber of commerce. The organization was struggling with financial solvency and had been brainstorming avenues for increasing revenues and membership. In my research on the organization, I couldn't identify a clearly articulated core ideology. As we began the session, I remarked that some of the struggles facing the organization likely trace back to the lack of a well-defined core ideology. Initially, we agreed that one of the focus areas of the strategic plan would be to create a mission statement.

As the initial meeting ended (we had scheduled three two-hour meetings to create the strategic plan), we started to discuss subcommittee assignments for the next meeting. It was agreed that we would do a SWOT analysis of the chamber's current state. It was then that a board member brought up a brilliant idea, one so perfect that I remember being pissed that I didn't think of it.

"Why don't we have our members do the SWOT analysis?"

You could have heard a pin drop. It is a bit scary to ask your customers to define your current state. However, I think you can make a compelling argument that they know better than you. You can tell the market who you are; but if they view you otherwise, I would suggest that you are wrong and *they* are right. Who better to tell us our strengths, weaknesses, opportunities, and threats than the people who were experiencing our services? As for me, after a career of promoting, training, and facilitating customer advisory boards, I just shook my head at the genius of the suggestion.

It does take some guts to invite your customers to perform a SWOT analysis on your organization – but you can't ask for a better way of getting some truly meaningful data on your current state. You don't need to facilitate a meeting with them to accomplish the SWOT analysis, either. By creating a simple survey, you can obtain ample evidence of your strengths, weaknesses, opportunities, and threats. For the chamber, it looked like this:

- What do you believe we do well as an organization?
- What do we currently do that you believe we could do better?
- What are we not doing that you believe would be beneficial if we did?
- What changes in your situation/direction could result in you not renewing your membership?

The answer to these questions will populate your SWOT analysis, respectively. You can wordsmith the questions to reflect the nature of your organization. Use Table 2.1 to get started.

Table 2.1   Basic SWOT Analysis

What do you believe we do well as an organization? (Strengths)	What do we currently do that you believe we could do better? (Weaknesses)
What are we not doing that you believe would be beneficial if we did? (Opportunities)	What changes in your situation/direction could result in you not renewing your membership? (Threats)

Determine the Desired Future State

Here, we let our freak flags fly. What do we need to be as an organization? I have found two approaches to be effective: one is aspirational and the other reflective. The aspirational approach posits that we should be unencumbered by what we are today and imagine a future state that exists in a perfect world. This is a lot of fun because it allows participants to completely reimagine the organization. But obviously, a complete rebuild of the organization can be time consuming and impractical, so this approach doesn't always make sense.

However, what if the group answered that third question – "Are there products/services that do not currently exist that would meet the needs of the marketplace or create a new desire?" – with some exciting possibilities? If so, one can certainly imagine engaging in an aspirational future state that addresses this new product/service that does not exist in the market environment.

The reflective approach turns the SWOT analysis around to create a TOWS analysis. A TOWS analysis is a lesser-known resource that plays the components of the SWOT analysis off each other. Executing a TOWS analysis means discussing the following:

- How do our strengths position us to take advantage of our opportunities?

- How can our strengths protect us from threats?
- How do we minimize the effect of our weaknesses so we don't miss our opportunities?
- How do we eliminate or hide our weaknesses to avoid being damaged by threats?

While maybe not as much fun as the aspirational approach, the TOWS analysis will not only provide a substantive desired future state, but will also jumpstart the strategic plan.

Both approaches have their own strengths and weaknesses. The aspirational approach is long on vision and mission but can be short on strategy and completely bereft of initiatives and action items. There can be more than a few "we don't know what we don't know" moments. It is said that learning is a process of going from "I don't know what I don't know" to "I know what I don't know" to "I know what I know" to, finally, "I don't know what I know." Good strategic planning requires knowledge, so you must at least know what you don't know. To be completely clueless is not the basis for the development of a meaningful core ideology.

The reflective approach is long on strategy and mission, but short on vision. Most of the work is spent on knowing your current state and developing strategies to improve it. The desired future state is generally just a better version of the current state. But radical change isn't always – or often – necessary to coax peak performance out of an otherwise healthy organization. In his book *Good to Great*, author Jim Collins called this the flywheel effect where peak performance is the result of many little things (turns) that result in a breakthrough (the moment the flywheel releases its energy).

The aspirational approach often produces a bigger, broader, and more creative desired future state, putting even more pressure on developing strategy. The reflective approach will produce a more pragmatic vision but can be self-limiting. So – which should you use?

Will Our Core Ideology Be Reflective or Aspirational?

This issue comes up at nearly every core ideology facilitation workshop that I do. Should our core ideology reflect who we are today? Or should it be an aspiration that we have for organization? A reflective core ideology is based on identifying your "secret sauce" that has helped you become successful and articulating it in a vision, mission, and strategy more clearly. An aspirational core ideology is an admission that we need something different than we have now and that our vision, mission, and strategy must change to achieve our desired future state.

Essentially, the answer to this question will be determined by the current state of the organization. If executive leadership feels that we are doing the right things to achieve our desired future state, but we just haven't articulated a clear vision, mission, and strategy to guide our journey, then a reflective core ideology would be the best type. If the current core ideology will not drive us toward that desired future state, then we must aspire to a new one.

Honestly, the most common component of horizontal alignment that drives these considerations is the success scoreboard. To put a finer point on the subject, the most common measure in the success scoreboard that drives the decision is profitability. When an organization isn't making enough money, self-examination follows quickly – more quickly, unfortunately, than when other success scoreboard measures are missed. I don't mean that to sound cynical. In my 35 years in organizational development, every single organization-wide strategic planning process in which I have been involved was initiated due to fiscal concerns. It is what it is.

Of course, nothing is binary in human behavior and organizations are merely a collective of behaviors. You may find that some of your current core ideology makes sense, but that you will need to add some aspirational components to achieve that desired future state. Your SWOT analysis (described earlier in this chapter) can help determine if your approach should be reflective, aspirational, or a combination. If you find that you are building your core ideology around your strengths and weaknesses, then you are using a reflective approach. If your core ideology addresses your opportunities and threats, you are using an aspirational approach. If you are integrating all four elements, you are using a combination *and* you should probably expect the process to last longer than the time you allotted for it. The results can be quite surprising.

I'll Have the Combo Please

I recently worked with a roofing company near Detroit. This family-owned company had been successful for many years and had recently begun to diversify their services by acquiring an HVAC company and a metal fabrication facility. Their core ideology was dated and vague and did not include this expansion in capabilities.

Because of their current and historic success, it made sense to use a reflective approach. However, upon doing a SWOT analysis, it was obvious that both their strengths and their opportunities had changed due to the acquisitions. They thought of themselves as a roofing company that happened to own an HVAC company and had the unique ability to fabricate sheet metal in house. Additionally, they had forged many relationships with peripheral service providers because of their history in the market. By broadening their capabilities (adding HVAC and sheet metal fabrication) and deepening their resources (relationships with other specialty contractors), they could aspire to be a comprehensive facility solutions partner for their client.

Their mission statement became a combination of reflective and aspirational: "Our passion is building enduring partnerships around creative and comprehensive facility solutions." That is a far cry from just replacing your roof or fixing your air conditioning or making some ductwork. That's the power of a well-conceived aspirational approach to strategic planning.

It really goes back to that simple SWOT analysis. Again, if you are building off strengths and weaknesses, utilize a reflective approach to determining your core ideology. If you are focused on opportunities and threats, consider an aspirational approach to determining your core ideology. And be prepared to incorporate a little of both as the process evolves.

Generative Positions and Core Ideology

One last thought relating to the generative role of boards and executive leadership teams and their impact on core ideology. Core ideologies that represent the generative responsibility of the people steering the organization consider its legacy – the impact of the work on the generations that will follow – and systems to continually impact or initiate the changes required to respond to future states many years away. It combines the notion of generational – things that will impact the next generation of people – and generating – a process for continually understanding the changes in the market environment.

While noble, these core ideologies can be really, really hard to nail down. It will require a keen understanding of trends, technologies, and perspectives that will shape the future and craft a vision to positively influence the people and processes that will populate this world. The unvarnished truth is that most organizations are focused on the next fiscal quarter, maybe even month, rather than the next decade. Most generative elements of core ideologies to which I have been exposed are more akin to language that promotes the continual evaluation of the ever-changing variables that impact the market environment to be ahead of emerging trends.

Practically, generative core ideologies are a sort of long-term aspirational core ideology meant to address potential opportunities and threats that do not currently exist, but can be anticipated. Or they are a long-term reflective core ideology that imagines how the strengths and weaknesses that exist today can be applied in a changing world of the future. The common element is that it is a long-term view, beyond the one- to five-year time frame of a typical strategic plan. They serve to inspire the organization to think bigger and further ahead. On that level, they can be very impressive and inspirational. However, if the organization is still dealing with operational issues and just beginning to imagine a desired future state, engaging in long-range generative perspectives on core ideologies is likely biting off a bit too much for now.

Construct the Core Ideology

Armed with a unified leadership team, knowledge of the market environment, an identified organizational current state, and a desired organizational future state, you are now ready to construct your core ideology: vision, mission, and strategy. The vision is arguably the easiest since you have already identified a desired future state. It often only requires some wordsmithing to convert the language of the exercises to a single coherent image of the future.

Mission can be trickier. Many times, the mission does not change during a leadership retreat. Often, the group decides that the "why" we exist hasn't really changed. Other times, the mission does change, or it may be identified for the very first time, as was the case with that roofing company in Detroit. A good mission statement should be just that – a statement. Two sentences are acceptable, one sentence is better, a paragraph is too much. Simple is better, meaningfulness essential. A well-constructed mission statement becomes the basis for every business decision in a peak performance culture. Here are some mission statements/brand slogans from a few of my clients:

Doing Well and Doing Good

Piramal Inc.

≫

Building Homes to Live Your Dreams
>>> *William Lyon Homes*

≫

To provide businesses the opportunity to control their insurance costs through the creation and oversight of member-owned group captive insurance companies
>>> *Captive Resources*

≫

A String of Pearls
>>> *Ste Michelle Wine Estates*

≫

Simple and Rewarding Home Loan Experience
>>> *PrimeLending*

Finally, the strategic plan is developed. This is the most time-consuming and detailed part of the core ideology and will likely require additional work beyond the retreat. However, the leadership team must identify and agree upon high-level priorities for initiatives. You can worry about action plans, individual tasks, responsibilities, timelines, and metrics later. However, you must achieve consensus on the priorities of focus that will move the organization from current state to desired future state.

By process end, you will have been successful if you achieve:

- A more unified executive leadership team
- A better understanding of the market environment
- A clear identification of the organization's current state
- A clear identification of the organization's desired future state
- The construction of a core ideology (vision, mission, strategy) for achieving that future state

THE FIRST STEP OF ALIGNMENT IS DONE

Peak performance culture begins with a foundation of passion. However, passion without horizontal alignment can result in doing something well that need not be done at all. By aligning your core ideology snugly between the inputs of the market environment and the desired outputs of the success scoreboard, you are now well positioned for success. The examples of Cayuse and Sleight of Hand illustrate the importance of the core ideology.

While horizontal alignment is critical to the organization's success, it is not singular. The best core ideology is useless – even potentially dangerous – to the organization if it is not consistent with the policies, procedures and practices of the organization. That is vertical alignment – and that's what we'll tackle in the following chapter.

Key Considerations

- Horizontal alignment requires that an organization has a clear mechanism for ongoing evaluation of the market environment.

- It is essential that a "success scoreboard" has been constructed. This scoreboard should include expectations for fiscal achievement, operational efficiency, and stakeholder (ownership, customers and employees) satisfaction/retention.

- A core ideology defines the organizational vision, mission, and strategy and connects the market environment with the success scoreboard.

- A core ideology answers these questions: Who are we? Why would a customer choose us over our competitors? How do we deliver that?

- The formulation of a core ideology is the result of knowing your organization's current state, desired future state, and the strategy for achieving the latter from the former.

The Five Metrics of Peak Performance Culture

Horizontal Alignment: Executive Leadership Team Survey

For each statement, please assign a number from 1 to 5 according to this scale:

1 = Never true 2 = Rarely true 3 = About half the time 4 = Mostly true 5 = Always true

I feel comfortable offering my opinion during meetings.   _____

I am confident that all leadership team members are dedicated to the success of the organization.   _____

We can engage in spirited debate without fear of damaging relationships.   _____

Trust score

I am enthusiastic about my involvement on this team.   _____

All members of the leadership team contribute to our success.   _____

I am confident that my fellow team members are fully engaged during meetings.   _____

Engagement score

Leadership team meetings produce valuable ideas.   _____

I feel like my ideas for improving the organization are given due consideration.   _____

This team places an importance on anticipating and discussing potential challenges to the organization.   _____

Idea generation score

I enjoy working with my fellow team members.   _____

This team has a clear methodology for working together to solve problems.   _____

We leverage the individual skills and styles of our team members to arrive at the best solutions.   _____

Collaboration score

I know what is expected of me as a team member.   _____

All members display a clear understanding of their responsibilities to this team.   _____

We do a great job of explaining the role of this team within the organization.   _____

Clear expectations score

The Five Metrics of Peak Performance Culture
Horizontal Alignment: Nonprofit Boards

For each statement, please assign a number from 1 to 5 according to this scale:

**1 = Never true 2 = Rarely true 3 = About half the time 4 = Mostly true
5 = Always true**

I feel comfortable offering my opinion during board
meetings. _____

I am confident that all board members are dedicated to
the success of the organization. _____

We can engage in spirited debate without fear of
damaging relationships. _____

Trust score ☐

I am enthusiastic about my involvement on this board. _____

All members of the board contribute to our success as
an organization. _____

I am confident that my fellow board members are fully
engaged during meetings. _____

Engagement score ☐

Board and committee meetings provide an opportunity
to explore valuable ideas. _____

I feel like my ideas for impacting the organization's
mission are given due consideration. _____

This board places an importance on enhancing the
relevancy of the organization within the community. _____

Idea generation score ☐

I enjoy working with my fellow board members. _____

This board has a clear methodology for working
together to formulate a long-term strategy and
evaluate goal achievement. _____

We leverage the individual skills and styles of our board
to arrive at the best strategy. _____

Collaboration score ☐

I know what is expected of me as a board member. _____

All board members display a clear understanding of
their responsibilities to this board and organization. _____

We do a great job of explaining the role of this board
within the organization and community. _____

Clear expectations score ☐

Chapter 3 Vertical Alignment

Horizontal alignment is hard, but it is a far cry easier to achieve than vertical alignment. I have facilitated hundreds of strategic planning retreats with leaders of companies and associations for the purpose of creating stronger horizontal alignment. Within a week – and sometimes over the course of a single day – these events generate a well-articulated core ideology that reflects the executive team's understanding of the market and how to exist within it to generate the desired measures of success. While there have been a few exceptions over the years, most of these retreats have ended with team unity on this core ideology, enthusiasm for what it means for the organization, and a renewed vigor for the future. Yet within weeks of the event, much of this work will have been for naught due to a lack of vertical alignment.

Vertical alignment is much more complicated and time consuming than horizontal alignment. While horizontal alignment is a sort of leadership epistemology, vertical alignment is more akin to a leadership methodology. It is more tactical than strategic, though its origins are in the latter. Unlike horizontal alignment, vertical alignment is never static. Rather, it is a *continuous process* of identifying, adjusting, eliminating, and adding policies, procedures, and practices – starting with the most visible and influential and continuing through the subtle and innocuous. Vertical alignment requires tenacity, patience, attention to detail, stubbornness on matters of minutiae, and many other characteristics that rarely exist among senior leadership, and that executives do not often value in others. Horizontal alignment is about vision, concepts, and broad strategies. Vertical alignment is about initiatives and action plans. It involves tasks, assignments, deadlines, deliverables, and measurables.

You could say that horizontal alignment is deciding where you want to go on vacation, and vertical alignment is making the myriad arrangements necessary to take time off, vacate your house, and travel to and from a destination. The logistics can often suck the fun out of the idea. This is more evidence of the importance of passion to peak performance culture. Whereas horizontal alignment involves broad business issues like market analysis and trends and pertinent fiscal considerations like profitability, efficiency, and stakeholder satisfaction – topics that appeal to executives and can be addressed within a finite time period – vertical alignment deals with human resources policies, customer service techniques, experience mapping, merchandising, advertising campaigns, policy development, evaluation of practices, and the like. Some of these considerations may be of interest to specific executives, but most of the tasks will create what the Rolling Stones refer to as "Far Away Eyes" around the boardroom inhabitants. If you want to see a CEO's eyes glaze over in five seconds, start a sentence with "Let's talk about our attendance policy."

What makes this all so alarming is knowing how imperative vertical alignment is to generating peak performance. In fact, vertical alignment determines the organization's success or failure far more often than horizontal alignment. Horizontal alignment is the "talk." Vertical alignment is the "walk." Accomplishing both would be "walking the talk." Even the most mediocre executive leadership teams can arrive at a workable core ideology. However, that talk, without the walk, will be detrimental to peak performance. In fact, *not* "walking the talk" will be detrimental to operational excellence as the employees and customers discover that the core ideology is merely words and not actions. Conversely, vertically aligned companies, even with mediocre horizontal alignment, will continue to produce results.

Think of it like this. If you are a race car driver who is of average talent competing against other drivers with more talent, then you want to make sure that your car is the best it can be and remains that way throughout the race. Then you stay on the track, keep the car running at its best, and hope other cars break down or crash. You may not win the race, but you will finish ahead of most of your competitors because of a healthy car. A more talented driver with that same car will beat you, but a more talented driver with a defective car won't. In this analogy, horizontal alignment is the driver's talent; vertical alignment is the car. You can win a race occasionally by having enough talent and a good car. You won't win a race by having superior talent and a bad car. Of course, what you should aspire to is having the best driver in the best car! That is when horizontal alignment is coupled with vertical alignment.

Executives get excited about horizontal alignment. They order posters, create branding messages, hold employee meetings – all designed to promote their core ideology. A few months later, the excitement fades and we are left with the operational processes to propel the core ideology through the organization and into the market. Without these processes – the vertical alignment – the core ideology becomes an empty promise to the stakeholders. The only thing worse than a lack of horizontal alignment is having an expressed core ideology that is *not* reflected in the actual business approach displayed by the organization. And, truth be told, this is common. Of the five metrics of peak performance culture, vertical alignment is the least interesting, most challenging, most often overlooked, and – arguably – the most important. "Arguably" only because passion provides the foundation of peak performance culture, so it is hard to understate its importance. But even a passionate culture will have a difficult time overcoming an insufficient infrastructure.

VERTICAL ALIGNMENT SHOULDN'T BE AN AFTERTHOUGHT

A large reason for why vertical alignment is so difficult is that it is rarely considered until later in an organization's existence. As it relates to horizontal alignment, many new organizations recognize the need to arrive at a core ideology that resonates with the market and produces the desired success scoreboard. Of course, some don't, but if I were to ask the owner of a new company, "Have you thought about what makes your business better than the competition?" I would be surprised if they did not have an answer (even if it's not true). However, if I asked that owner, "How do your operational processes, principles, and practices support that competitive advantage?" I would expect a long, silent, melancholy gaze. Or just a shrug.

Policies are often established as a matter of necessity, legal guidance, or simply because "it seemed like something that we should have." They are often reactionary, installed after something bad has happened. They are not generally implemented as a strategic tool to drive our operation in alignment with our core ideology. They *should* be, but they are not. Most organizations approach policies and procedures as if they are completing a checklist rather than devising the tactical and strategic components of our core ideology.

A common evolution of the employee handbook is a great example of ineffective vertical alignment. Most employee handbooks began as a realization there was a problem with an employee that needed to be addressed – say a problem like attendance. One employee was calling in sick more frequently and/or at more inopportune moments than their co-workers. This leads to a conversation about a formal attendance policy. Then we arrive at an attendance policy. Then we have all employees read and sign the attendance policy. Then we realize we have several other issues for which we should have a policy. So we write policies for all these issues. We have the employees read and sign each of these policies. Over time, we identify other issues and we revise old policies that are ineffective, illegal, or silly. Then we decide to put all these policies in one handbook so all new employees can read and sign them. This process can take years, and not one time did we ask ourselves if any of these policies support the core ideology of the organization. What we have is a handbook (check) that addresses attendance (check), dress code (check), performance reviews (check), employee discipline (check), promotions (check), compensation and benefits (check), personal days (check), and so on. The checklist is complete, and the employee handbook is done. And yet, we are not vertically aligned with our core ideology.

After years of adding policies without consideration of their impact on our core ideology, we also have the variable of well-meaning, mid-level leaders who are applying these policies in their own unique way. After all, humans perceive things uniquely based on their experiences – ambiguous policies are ripe for varied interpretations. We also have executives who exist outside the influence of these policies. In many organizations, executive leadership members behave in ways outside the organization's policies. And we have many more company practices that are not reflected by expressed policies but that have a huge impact on the employee and/or customer experience. All these factors are now conspiring to misalign the organization, short circuit the vehicle of peak performance, and undermine the core ideology. Even the most talented race car driver can't coax a Ford Pinto into the winner's circle. (All apologies to any Ford Pinto owners.)

By the time an organization realizes that they are not vertically aligned, the job of correcting this misalignment can seem hopelessly daunting. "Where do we begin?" I often hear from clients with more than a subtle amount of desperation in their tone. Good news! I have a suggestion and it involves the unintended consequences of a federal civil rights law and that dusty three-ring binder that sits in every department.

THE INCREDIBLE VALUE OF A WELL-DESIGNED JOB DESCRIPTION

When the Americans with Disabilities Act (ADA) of 1990 became a law, it introduced some important new requirements for employers, including "reasonable accommodations." *Reasonable accommodations* became a legal term referring to the adjustments (and costs) that an employer must consider and incur to allow an otherwise qualified disabled candidate to perform the essential functions of a job. As employers navigated the legal requirements of this law, they were encouraged to revisit that archaic form in each department – the job description. These job descriptions were enhanced to include a list of the essential functions, job responsibilities that could be accommodated and how, and any specific physical, mental, and emotional capabilities required to do the job. At the time, this was a colossal project for companies, and most approached it like the creation of the employee handbook – another checklist item.

The peak performance organization saw this as an opportunity. Think about what a job description really is. It is not just a list of the work that is required in a specific job title. The job description is a document that provides the reason and evidence for why this position exists within the organization and how it supports the core ideology. It links every single job within the organization to the core ideology. There is no better single document in a company to propel vertical alignment.

As such, the job description should contain the following:

- What is the job title?
- Why is this job title necessary to support our core ideology?
- What education, skills, and experience are needed to perform this job at the entry level?

- Where will this job title exist within the organization (depiction on organizational chart)?
- How will this job title interact with others within the organization?
- What tasks are required within this job title and how do they relate to core ideology?
- How well must one perform these tasks to meet the expected standard?
- What skills are required to perform each of these tasks?
- What behaviors are expected related to the organizational handbook?
- What level of authority/decision making is allowed?
- When and with whom does this job title need to report?

With each of these components identified for the job title, you can now use this description to generate the following:

- Talent recruiting and acquisition strategies
- Targeted employment interview questions for talent selection
- Organizational orientation for new hires
- New hire skill training programs
- Performance feedback processes
- Employee coaching and counseling plans
- Professional development and career path planning
- Merit increase philosophies
- Succession planning strategies

That's a lot of alignment generated by one well-designed document. Unfortunately, many organizations don't even know where their job descriptions are and haven't referred to them since, well, 1990. Organizations under 20 people may not need to comply with the ADA and therefore have never developed job descriptions at all. At least for these companies, the project of creating job descriptions isn't so large. For larger firms that have not updated the job descriptions in thirty years, the thought of digging them up and starting virtually from scratch is far from appealing, hence why vertical alignment is so difficult. The temptation is to try to patch it rather than fix it. This approach is counterproductive in that the patch only adds more complexity to an already needlessly complicated system. This leads to further inefficiency, which steers us away from another critical component of our success scoreboard. Vertically misaligned organizations experience the negative consequences in all elements of the success scoreboard: profitability, efficiency, and stakeholder satisfaction.

A MISALIGNED BRAND

After completing the massive undertaking of enhancing every job description in the organization so it reflects the approach listed above, then comes the only slightly less overwhelming project of evaluating the consistent execution of all policies, procedures, and practices in the organization to assess their vertical alignment to the core ideology. To accomplish this, it is essential to consider how your organization is structured and where misalignment can occur. Consider Figure 3.1, which incorporates vertical alignment with horizontal alignment.

The most damaging misalignment would occur at the organizational level. This means that you are applying a policy, procedure, or practice across the breadth of the entire company that is not aligned with the core ideology of the organization. This sounds difficult to imagine, but it is quite common. Let me give you an example.

Imagine that you are a client of an organization that states that customer satisfaction is their top priority. That sounds familiar, right? Many companies express a core ideology that claims to elevate the customer's needs to the center of their attention – customer centricity is their mantra. However, let's also imagine that you have purchased a product from this

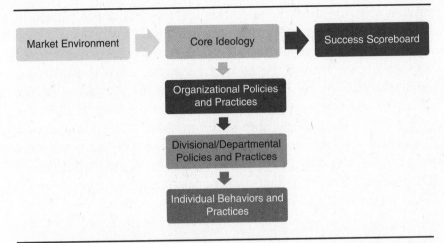

FIGURE 3.1   The intersection of vertical alignment and horizontal alignment.

company that has failed to meet your expectations. It's not defective, just not exactly what you were looking for.

Unfortunately, between your recent vacation and a bit of chaos upon your return, you didn't discover the product shortcomings for a few weeks. It happens, no problem; you will simply contact the company on their convenient toll-free customer service hotline. You listen to the automated voice explain the six alternatives you can select to more effectively route your call. None sound like the exact fit for your needs, so you select 0 to speak to a customer service representative.

After a less than reassuring 10-minute wait on hold for that customer service representative, during which you were repeatedly serenaded by a bad rendition of "The Girl from Ipanema," you are grilled for all the necessary information related to your purchase. You know, that whole "order number, product, date of purchase, nature of concern" inquisition? Sadly, it turns out you are two days beyond the return allowance. Darn the luck. But stay on the line for the brief customer satisfaction survey and special offer. You will never get those 30 minutes back.

Most readers can relate to this story. This is a classic example of vertical misalignment at the organizational level. In fact, we have a few: the automated phone service that doesn't quite fit the customer needs; the long wait on hold to speak to a customer service representative; the denial of the return due to an arbitrary time frame; the lack of recourse when the outcome isn't satisfactory. All these policies are contrary to the core ideology of customer centricity. It would almost be easier for the company to change the core ideology from "Your satisfaction is our top priority" to something more like "We hope you like what you bought because things get complicated otherwise." Or maybe, "Your satisfaction is occasionally our top priority." That seems fair, and more accurate.

DIGGING DEEPER INTO ALIGNMENT

It's important to evaluate not just an organization's *expressed* policies and procedures, but their practices, too. Practices refer to what employees are doing within the organization regardless of the actual policy and procedure. It is especially common when evaluating divisional/departmental differences (which can extend across cultures and geographies as well as functional responsibilities) and even more so among individuals within the organization. While organizational misalignment has a wide impact on the organization, divisional/departmental and individual misalignment will alienate customers and employees, too. And these can be even harder to uncover. One misaligned employee can create a lot of performance damage for the organization before they are identified. This is particularly true if the entire organization is misaligned. On the other hand, the more vertically aligned the organization becomes, the more obvious any form of misalignment becomes.

Here are a couple of examples for departmental and individual misalignment that I have experienced. The first involves the use of personal time (paid days off for vacation, illness, or other approved reasons). I find this policy to be consistently well defined and communicated at the organizational level. It usually involves the identification of a specific number of days allotted each year depending on the employee's length of employment. For example, the company may provide 10 days of personal time after one year of employment. The policy will likely outline the procedure for requesting those days and/or using the personal time for an absence. If an employee wishes to take vacation, for example, they may need to request time off one month in advance. If an employee misses work due to an illness, they may be required to bring a doctor's note upon return or to have notified work before the start of their shift or some other stipulation outlined in the policy. Whatever the details, the key is that the company has designed a specific approach to accumulating and using personal time.

So far, so good. We have a well-defined policy and procedure at the organization level. However, what if one department within the company becomes lax in their enforcement of that policy? Let's say the sales department has a habit of allowing their sales representatives to leave at noon on Friday if they have reached their sales goal. Further, let's say that this half day off is still paid without dipping into employees' personal time accrual. This creates a misalignment in the organization, since some employees now benefit by a different application of a policy than others. If you think this doesn't impact employee satisfaction, I can assure you it does. I spent countless hours in my human resources roles trying to defend the differences in policy practices between departments. Inequities in the employee experience – a topic we will explore in more detail later – always lead to dissatisfaction. This in turn impacts the customer experience and. . .well, you see the problem.

Individual behaviors are the most common form of misalignment and easiest to address if leadership remains committed to good coaching and performance feedback practices. Misaligned individual behavior is reflected in any situation during which the employee engages in an activity or policy practice that is contrary to the organization's procedure. For example, using the customer-centric example from above, the employee who summarily dismissed the return because it fell outside the time limit for product refunds was displaying a misaligned behavior.

In that example, the behavior may have been created by misaligned policies at the department or organizational level. If the company or department policy was that all returns must be completed within 30 days to receive a full refund with no recourse for customers at all, I would argue that the policy is *not* customercentric. If, on the other hand, there was no such policy or one that stated that exceptions can be made by involving a supervisor, then the employee's behavior was misaligned. If it is simply an individual employee behavior, coaching or counseling should fix the problem. But if it is a department practice misalignment, changes must be made at that level and all employees within that department retrained. If the organizational policy is misaligned, the entire company would need retraining on a more customercentric procedure. That's why it is so important to work top down on vertical alignment and with an abundance of passion to sustain the effort.

There is good news. Your continued efforts at vertical alignment will create momentum. As things align around your core ideology, it's easier to identify which practices and policies are not aligned. It is almost as if vertical misalignment provides a cloaking effect on poor performance. Once you start removing the misalignment, performance inhibitors become easier to detect and correct. It all revolves around evaluating every policy, procedure, practice, and behavior relative to how they impact the core ideology of the organization.

But what if the misalignment begins before your customer even experiences your policies and procedures? Is that possible? Unfortunately, it is not just possible, but common.

THE MISALIGNED SALES PROCESS

I teach selling skills. Wait, let me correct that statement. I teach a specific approach to business development called consultative selling. Consultative selling is a form of sales that works well within a customer centric core ideology. At least as I define consultative selling, this form of business development requires that the sales professional understand two distinct things about their consumer *before* they recommend products and/or services to them.

First, it is important to understand what type of communication/relationship/rapport the customer wants from their sales professional. Do they want a friend, a problem solver, a product specialist, an idea person? All of these may sound good, but the reality is the consumer is most comfortable with just one of these types as partners. Understanding that about the consumer will allow the sales professional to tailor their conversations and recommendations appropriately. For more information on this topic, please pick up a copy of my book *The Power of Understanding People*. I also touch on this in the chapter on customer experience.

Once the nature of the relationship has been identified, the successful consultative sales professional will ask the appropriate questions to uncover the client's expressed and unexpressed needs. Expressed needs are the ones that the customer articulates to the sales professional. For example, when buying a refrigerator, a customer may express the need for a specific size, color, and style (freezer and refrigerator side by side, for instance). The unexpressed needs are the ones that the customer may not realize they have but that the sales professional uncovers based on their knowledge of the products/services they provide and familiarity with the field in which they work. Continuing the refrigerator example, the salesperson may identify the importance of an in-the-door ice and water dispenser and wine chilling drawer because the customer frequently entertains others. Once the sales professional understands both the relationship needs of their customer and the critical needs for products/services based on their situation, they are now able to offer the appropriate solutions to the client for addressing these needs.

My point here is not to educate you on how consultative selling works, but rather to establish the foundation for what a misaligned sales process looks like. Let's just say that, on more than one occasion over the last 25 years or so, I have conducted consultative sales training at the request of an organization's executive leadership. This sometimes involved several days' worth of education and practice to ensure the attendees understand how to successfully identify client communication styles, how to establish rapport with those various styles, and what questions to ask to identify critical needs. We focus on bridging the client's critical needs to the company's capabilities– a process I call "framing the value." We even spend significant time on maintaining a collaborative relationship while addressing customer concerns. It is a rigorous, but ultimately fulfilling, vocational education experience.

And then after my training the marketing department unveils the new 50 slide PowerPoint sales deck to be presented *as is* to each client: a deck that begins with "Our History" introduces the products/services on slides 10–40, addresses "Common Concerns" for 5 slides, and closes with a generic slide that says "Questions?" What the fork, man?

There is nothing remotely consultative about having a one-size-fits-all PowerPoint sales presentation deck that attempts to address all types of consumers, explains all our products and services, reduces individual concerns to common concerns, and only allows for questions after the 60 minute "death by PPT."

Now, my point here isn't that I think a consultative selling approach is a better business model (I do); but why in the world would you claim a core ideology of customercentricity, spend several days training your business development team on consultative selling, and then provide them with a sales tool that is distinctively product/services centric? Either you need to change your core ideology and sales training or burn the sales presentation PowerPoint deck. I think you know my vote.

The most common customer complaint I have heard as it relates to a company's vertical alignment is that the way the company was represented by the sales professional has little resemblance to the actual customer experience. We will examine the role of customer experience in a future chapter, but if the organization is vertically aligned around a core ideology that is not reflected in the business development process, then the whole thing gets wonky real fast. Essentially, you have misrepresented the organization to the consumer. And when that happens, good luck achieving customer satisfaction (and forget about retention).

The most successful organizations not only have well-aligned business development processes; they also make sure the sales professionals stay actively involved in the client experience as they move through the operation. If you want to know how well aligned you are vertically as an organization, ask your customer. And who usually finds out first if you are not aligned? The sales professional. Peak performing organizations have business development teams that also serve as organizational development consultants, because they are the ones who get the call from the unhappy customer.

BRAND STATEMENT AND VERTICAL ALIGNMENT

I enjoy working with marketing professionals. Heck, my daughter is a marketing professional. They are often among the most positive, creative, and immediately likable people I meet within organizations. They have a *very* important role in organizational success. And it is this fact – that marketing is so important to our success as an organization – that results in the pressure to construct a brand story that may not reflect the true capabilities of the organization.

I know this is not a malicious endeavor – it's not like the marketing department has a weekly "How Do We Make False Promises That Resonate with Our Customers" meeting on Tuesdays (although that does sound like a funny *Saturday Night Live* bit). There exist tremendous demands to distinguish ourselves in a crowded market. Sometimes this results in the creation of brand statements that are based far more on how they poll with customers rather than how accurately they reflect the organization's true capabilities and strengths.

If your organization is representing capabilities or experiences that it cannot deliver on, you are misaligned vertically.

The best organizations – the peak performers – make a brand promise that accurately reflects the deliverables to the customer. One of the easiest ways to assess an organization's commitment to vertical alignment is to look at the customer feedback process. First, do they have one? Many don't. Second, what are you asking your customer to rate? And are the things they are rating really that important to *them*? Later, in the chapter on customer experience, we will examine the importance of knowing what will *retain* your clients, not just satisfy them. Your core ideology, when vertically aligned throughout the organization, must deliver those elements to your customer.

Major corporations are certainly capable of identifying and delivering on a brand promise. One of my favorite clients is Allstate Insurance. "You're in good hands with Allstate" goes the brand slogan. Having worked with several of their claim centers over the course of many years, I can confirm that they are populated by employees who are emotionally sensitive, tactful, self-sacrificing, and genuinely driven by a desire to help others. There is clear evidence that the company policies are designed to identify, hire, and train people who will contribute to a policyholder experience that reflects their brand slogan. That is an example of vertical alignment.

Customer satisfaction as a metric is about delivering on your brand promise. The brand promise should be a source of competitive advantage and a direct extension of the core ideology and horizontal alignment. Vertical alignment ensures that your brand promise is reflected in the policies, procedures, and practices at every level of the organization. We will revisit this again in the chapter on customer experience.

THE FALLACY OF "DISRUPTION"

One of the recurring challenges that I have witnessed in organizations around the world is the sudden urge to alter the organization's core ideology (horizontal alignment) without considering the accompanying changes required in vertical alignment. Over the last handful of years, the term "disruption" has become a popular buzz word in business. An evolution of the 1990s business concept known as disruptive technology, the more generic "disruption" approach is simpler and more straightforward. Many executives who embrace the creation of disruption are trying to avoid organizational complacency. They believe it is necessary to shake up the company with new core ideologies that will reinvigorate performance, generate enthusiasm among stakeholders, and recapture the excitement and commitment associated with the early stages of an organization's existence. All these things may happen. It is also possible that the disruption will cause what disruptions often cause: confusion. Successful disruption requires vertically aligned leadership. In other words, truly effective disruption is thoughtful, strategic, tactical, well planned. and executed. But that just doesn't sound like fun to the disruptor, who may be exhibiting one of the leadership toxins I discuss in Chapter 4.

It's not that changes are not ever necessary at a horizontal alignment level, because they are. It's just that these changes must be justified based on the market environment and then accompanied by the necessary adjustments in vertical alignment. They cannot simply be changes for the sake of "disrupting."

SMALL CHANGES IN HORIZONTAL ALIGNMENT CREATE *BIG* CHANGES IN VERTICAL ALIGNMENT

Recently, I was consulting with a global pharmaceutical company that had experienced a five-year run of revenue growth due in part to a new core ideology of customer centricity. The CEO believed that reaching a new level of success would require another change to the core ideology. In my experiences, most CEOs lead with a style I label as Adventurer (Mastermind/Warrior) or Power Broker (Warrior/Mastermind). You can refer to my two previous books for more information on interactive styles. I also discuss this briefly in the chapter that follows this one, "Leadership Ideology." But to sum up here:

Masterminds, by nature, grow bored with the status quo and seek change even if there is no indication it is necessary. Warriors are competitive and are always seeking an advantage. When you combine those two preferences, you create a mindset that requires a new idea to give yourself a competitive edge. The CEO of this organization was exactly this style of leader.

The company provides drug discovery, development, and manufacturing services to other pharmaceutical companies on a contractual basis. In a nutshell, pharma companies outsource parts of their work to my client. Their customer-centric ideology meant that they continually consider the client company's perspective, needs, and expectations as they provide the contracted services. The CEO proposed a change to this ideology from customercentric to patientcentric. This meant that the company would shift from a consultative relationship with their clients to a collaborative one. It was a subtle change – at least in the CEO's mind. These can be the most dangerous situations – the belief that the small change at the very top of the horizontal alignment requires only a tiny adjustment of vertical alignment throughout the company. However, anyone who has navigated a boat, built a house, or even tried to draw two parallel lines has come to appreciate how a slight adjustment at one end of an alignment can create a large movement at the other end.

Once the new core ideology had been articulated, it was important to quantify the exact impact this shift in the client relationship would have on the operation. The organization comprised several sites scattered around North America, Europe, and India. Each of these facilities was led by a site director and a leadership team. As is common in pharma, many of these facilities had been parts of different companies in the past and had been acquired by the current company. In a perfect world, each facility would have the exact same capabilities and expertise. This is not a perfect world. Each site had its own strengths and vulnerabilities. This, of course, created challenges to vertical alignment.

The business development (BD) team was trained to work with all the facilities. Given that BD was the first point of contact with the client and communicated this information to operations, it made sense to clearly define how the new patient centricity core ideology would affect their approach to the market. Of note was the fact that this organization was driven by a high-performing business development team. We decided to drive the core ideology shift through BD. A major hurdle to implementing the new core ideology was the success of the old core ideology. Since the customer centric approach had resulted in record revenue gains, why the need for a shift to patient centricity, they asked. Nothing alienates sales professionals as much as changing something that was making them money.

The vertical alignment efforts for this project began with a daylong examination of exactly what this shift from customer (pharma company) to patient (end user) centricity would mean relative to the efforts of BD. Herein lies the value of having these conversations deeper within the organization than just the C suite. After spirited discussion – and dissent – we achieved a breakthrough. If our customers are focused on the patient, and we profess to be customer centric, wouldn't that mean that we too must be *patient* centric? Was this really a shift in ideology or, more accurately, a sharpening of our focus? As we talk with our clients, shouldn't we know about their customers – the patient? The answers to these questions allowed the team to align around the revised core ideology. Patient centricity is simply a more refined version of customer centricity.

The breakthrough happened when we produced a visual that illustrated the change graphically. The company had visually represented their customer-centric approach by showing all the various business functions surrounding the customer. Realizing that the customer's customer was the patient, that placed the patient in the center of the customer's focus (reflected by the additional oval within the customer centricity graphic in Figure 3.2). The BD team was satisfied that this "sharper focus" of our core ideology would not negatively impact their

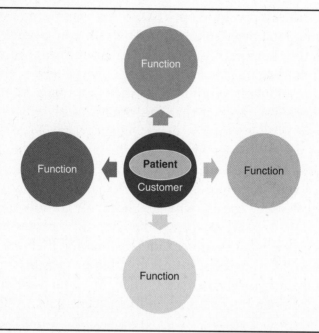

FIGURE 3.2   Sharpening the core ideology from customer to patient.

relationships with clients. With that, we were ready to drive the ideology deeper in the organization.

Simultaneous to this, all C-suite leaders needed to clearly understand the impact of patient centricity in their disciplines. Each organization-wide policy and practice would need to be evaluated for its impact on patient centricity. Divisional and departmental practice would then need to be addressed – BD and site operations needed to understand how this new collaborative relationship would work between clients and the organization, and between BD and operations. Once they determined this, each department within the global sites needed to adjust their policies and practices accordingly to integrate this sharper focus. For example, cross-functional Patient Awareness Councils were formed at each site to reflect this new ideology (customer awareness councils are discussed in Chapter 5, "The Customer Experience"). Finally, policies and practices impacting individual employees – things like job descriptions, training, appraisal criteria – would require modification to reflect this "subtle change."

The point here is that any change to the organization's core ideology, no matter how small it may seem, will have dramatic impact on vertical alignment at all levels of the company. When it comes to vertical alignment, all changes are disruptive!

Here's the thing: vertical alignment is hard work and it is not the hard work that you do every day. Few organizations fully realize the immense effort required to align the entire company around a core ideology. Combine that with the possibility that leadership changes these ideologies without considering the trickle-down impact of their decisions, and you come to understand why so few companies are vertically aligned. But the best organizations are either vertically aligned or continually in the process of achieving it. Peak-performing cultures walk the talk of their expressed core ideology.

VERTICAL ALIGNMENT AT THE DIVISIONAL/ DEPARTMENTAL LEVEL

Not all vertical alignment efforts start at the organization-wide level. In fact, many of the performance enhancement and strategic planning events that I have worked on with clients have been at the department level. The most common departmental level vertical alignment project revolves around communication. In the famous words of Strother Martin in the movie *Cool Hand Luke*, "What we have here is a failure to communicate." It is hard to achieve vertical alignment in a perfect situation, and impossible if the communication systems within a department are faulty.

There is good news, though. As vertical alignment efforts move deeper into the operation, from organizational to departmental, the misalignment often becomes more obvious, easier to define, and less complicated. Take communication, for example. Organization-wide communication problems are *much* harder to identify, define, and fix than a communication problem in one department. Once you identify a misalignment, the specific process that I have found to be beneficial for returning to alignment mirrors the approach we used to achieve horizontal alignment.

Step One: Identify Your Current State

This strategic planning technique is often employed when addressing *big* issues like core ideology or financial projections like the example we used in the last chapter on horizontal alignment, but it is also quite useful on more specific issues.

Take a departmental/divisional communication problem, for example. There are reasons that the department communication is the way it is. While it may be misaligned with the organization's core ideology, and perhaps even toxic, it evolved to this for a reason. As it relates to any practice, understanding the value, toxicity, and areas to improve represents the first step toward enhancing and aligning this practice. The gold standard for evaluating these things relative to a practice is that good old SWOT analysis. We used it for determining our current organizational state, and we can use it to determine our current departmental state.

To review, SWOT is an acronym for Strengths, Weaknesses, Opportunities, and Threats. To determine the current state of department communication, list the descriptors for each of these four topics. In the last chapter, we applied the SWOT analysis to the organization for horizontal alignment. Table 3.1 shows an example from a recent client using SWOT analysis to address communication within a single department for vertical alignment.

The value of performing a SWOT analysis is twofold. Not only do you identify the current state relative to the misaligned issue, you also achieve consensus on that current state. As it relates to communication, you could argue that achieving consensus on the issue is even more important. It serves as a team building function. By agreeing on the current state of a vertical

Table 3.1   SWOT Analysis Example

What Is the Current State of Communication Within Our Division?

Strengths	Weaknesses
• Everyone embraces core ideology.	• It's hard to find a schedule to assemble as a team.
• Peer-to-peer communication is strong.	• Criticizing leadership can be uncomfortable.
• Everyone is comfortable with their own function.	• The team doesn't communicate across functions effectively.
Opportunities	**Threats**
• If we knew more about other functions, we could avoid unintentional operational conflicts.	• Problems can get worse because not everyone is aware they exist.
• Team members can cross train in different functions.	• When we lose employees, no one can step in to do their work effectively.
• Better understanding of the entire operation can result.	• Bad decisions can be made because of a lack of awareness of impact on other functions.

misalignment issue, you have begun to better align it. Performance is already improving.

Step Two: Identify the Desired Future State

I approach this in a couple of different ways. For some issues and some departments, the act of completing a SWOT analysis provides enough clarity on the process to generate a healthy dialog about the desired future state. The client with communication issues outlined in the SWOT analysis above was able to create a desired future state immediately after

Table 3.2   TOWS Analysis Example

	Strengths	Weaknesses
	• Everyone embraces core ideology. • Peer to peer communication is strong. • Everyone is comfortable with their own function.	• It's hard to find a schedule to assemble as a team. • Criticizing leadership can be uncomfortable. • The team doesn't communicate across functions effectively.
Opportunities If we knew more about other functions, we could avoid unintentional operational conflicts. Team members can cross train in different functions. Better understanding of the entire operation can result.	*How do we use our strengths to take advantage of our opportunities?*	*How can we use our opportunities to reduce or minimize our weaknesses?*
Threats • Problems can get worse because not everyone is aware they exist. • When we lose employees, no one can step in to do their work effectively. • Bad decisions can be made because of a lack of awareness of impact on other functions.	*How do we use our strengths to protect against our threats?*	*How can we reduce or eliminate our threats by minimizing our weaknesses?*

completing the SWOT. They assigned cross-functional task forces to address their opportunities and threats.

Some departments/issues require the TOWS analysis step. As we discussed in Chapter 2, the TOWS analysis involves answering four questions:

- How do our strengths position us to take advantage of our opportunities?
- How can our strengths protect us from threats?
- How do we minimize the effect of our weaknesses so we don't miss our opportunities?
- How do we eliminate or hide our weaknesses to avoid being damaged by threats?

The completed TOWS analysis will provide the framework for the actionable items necessary to achieve the desired future state. Whether you arrive at the desired future state organically by doing just a SWOT analysis and assigning focus groups to address the details or by answering the four questions of the TOWS analysis, you'll need to complete one last step.

Step Three: Will the New Practice Align with the Organization's Core Ideology?

Remember, the entire process began because a departmental (or divisional) practice was identified as misaligned. It is entirely possible to go through the strategic planning process and arrive at a new practice that also does not align with the core ideology. So, before any tasks are assigned or celebratory champagne is popped, be sure to ask, "Will this align with our core ideology?"

PASSION IS THE FOUNDATION, ALIGNMENT IS THE INFRASTRUCTURE

Both horizontal and vertical alignment are ongoing efforts that require constant monitoring and corrective actions. It is important not to get frustrated by the never-ending effort that it takes. No organization is perfectly aligned. However, the best organizations are continuously engaged in the pursuit of alignment. They realize it is the cornerstone of organizational development. It is the infrastructure of peak performance culture and for that reason, it is impossible to achieve the full potential of an organization without it. Passion provides the foundation on which alignment builds the frame. Yet despite the importance of both passion and alignment, the metric that is most immediately noticeable in an organization, particularly for the employee population, is its leadership ideology. (More to come on that in Chapter 4.)

Key Considerations

- Vertical alignment begins with a clear organizational core ideology that is horizontally aligned with the market environment and the success scoreboard.
- Vertical alignment refers to every policy, procedure, and practice at the organizational, divisional/departmental, and individual level that supports the core ideology of the organization.
- Job descriptions are a particularly useful tool for generating vertical alignment because they can impact hiring, training, and appraisal.
- High-profile areas to address as it relates to vertical alignment are the sales process, the brand statement, leadership directives, and departmental/divisional communication.
- Activities and tools like SWOT analysis, TOWS analysis, and the identification of both the current state and desired future state of organizational practices are essential to fixing misalignment on both a horizontal and a vertical level.

Chapter 4 Leadership Ideology

It should not surprise you too much that an individual who started a company called the Leadership Difference, Inc. places a high level of importance on leadership when predicting organizational success. In fact, of the five metrics discussed in this book, leadership ideology is the only one that can, by itself, actually *will* a company to success. Leadership is that important – combined with passion, that is. If passion is an organization's foundation and alignment is its framework, leadership is the power. Like electricity in a house, leadership allows us the necessary source of all our company's potential. Due to my fixation with and focus on leadership, no other element of peak performance draws as much scrutiny from me when I work with an organization. And no other metric disappoints me as much as leadership when it is hamstringing organizational success.

Unfortunately, I have found it far too common that organizations struggle with leadership instead of excelling. I have often noticed that companies are created as a reflection of a single person's passion – someone who is inspired to lead others based on their own dedication to the success of an idea. They experience initial success, which requires that they expand the responsibility for leading the organization to others. Slowly, the passion, ideology and character that drove that initial success becomes diluted. The energy changes. While this may not be a terminal problem – many organizations continue to chug, stumble, and/or stagger along – the level of success of those early years is never replicated.

THE PROBLEM WITH VALUES

One clear symptom of an organization desperately trying to rekindle that original feeling is the identification of organizational values. You know, that list of 4–8 behaviors that the company believes is the cultural basis of their success and that they encourage, maybe even mandate, all employees to manifest. I have seen them hundreds of times, on websites ("About Us"), marketing materials ("Why Us?"), and – the most ridiculous of all – on posters in the employee cafeteria.

There I am, walking from the reception area to the CEO's office, human resources department, or training meeting room, and we pass a poster on the wall. It has been there for so long that it has become invisible to the employees, but it is new to me. The language is nearly the same wherever I go: "At ABC Dynamics, each employee embodies our values: Integrity, Honesty, Care, Dedication, and Accountability." The exact words change a little, although I am always struck by how often "integrity" and "honesty" make the short list. My reaction is always the same, "Do we really have to communicate to our employees that we value integrity?" "Isn't honesty something we should just expect rather than promote?" "Why would I employ someone who doesn't care, isn't dedicated, or lacks accountability?" And finally, "How many people have read this poster and thought to themselves, 'Well, I have not been honest in the past, but now that I know it is an organizational value, I will be honest going forward.'"

It's not that I don't see the value in behaviors like honesty, accountability, integrity, and so on; in fact, it is the opposite.

I hope all people believe in these values. I would think we would want to hire people who exhibit these characteristics. The ugly truth is, if a person does not possess these behaviors by – oh, I don't know – 25 years old, I doubt they ever will. And even if you could instill within them these values, is that really where you want to spend your time as a leader? That's called parenting, not leading.

I have always subscribed to a simple philosophy when it comes to selecting employees: hire character, train skills, lead style. The reason is straightforward. If a person is a combination of their character, their skills, and their style, you can only significantly change one of those through leadership. Thoughtful, thorough, and effective skill training will improve someone's talent. Style can certainly change over the course of a person's life. I have written two books on the topic: *The Power of Understanding People* and *The Power of Understanding Yourself*. Our style can transform as we amass new and different life experiences. Our job as leaders, however, is to recognize a person's style, communicate with them accordingly, and ensure that their intrinsic needs are met to promote peak performance (more on that later). It is not our responsibility to change someone's style. It is rarely necessary to do so.

Character is the element of a person's essence that we are least likely to change once they have reached adulthood. I assume it is possible – I would hate to give up on another person – but I would rather not be responsible for it as an employer. If someone is not honest, I don't want to have to invest time, money, and other resources trying to change their behaviors with no guarantee I will be successful. Imagine the damage this person is doing to customers and co-workers while I endeavor to teach them the importance of not lying. It sounds silly, right? And yet, there's that poster in the employee cafeteria.

But that isn't even the worst part of the company values poster. That poster, the one that lists honesty as one of the core values of the organization, is *itself* a lie. Not always, but often. I have worked with a lot of executives who don't reflect the values listed on their company's own website. I have sat in meetings with employees who have asked me why, if these values are so damn important, do their leaders not display them. It is uncomfortable because there is no defense for this situation.

Here's the problem. Life is complicated. What one person believes to be honesty, integrity, and dedication others view as something else. It is very difficult for us to agree on exactly what these things look like in every situation, and so they are quickly ineffectual. Worse, they are harmful in that they profess to create a specific expectation of behavior that can never be adequately fulfilled. The corporate values on that poster set you up for failure.

THE IMPORTANCE OF BEHAVIORS

This is not to say that there are *no* behaviors around which to build your culture. There are, and they begin with leadership. Specifically, I believe the leaders of the most successful organizations share a fundamental approach to how they lead. Steve Thompson, president of PrimeLending, shared with me some very impactful ideas on leadership ideology that have contributed to his organization's success. Two practices particularly struck me as uncommon in businesses. One was "assume positive intent." Many leaders, Thompson points out, can be quick to assume that mistakes are made for reasons other than the best interests of the organization or the people involved, whether that's a customer or an employee. The reality is that most employees are working hard to do what is right. Rather than immediately responding critically to errors in judgment, it is beneficial for leaders to "listen intently and be slow to respond in an attempt to first understand," says Thompson.

Related to assuming positive intent is leading with an "assume you don't know" mindset. Thompson describes the tendency of some leaders to presume an understanding of situations and make determinations for handling them before they have acquired all the information. By entering a conversation with the presumption of ignorance rather than omniscience, leaders often discover many more complexities involved in scenarios and can make even better decisions while also enhancing employee relations. Both "assume positive intent" and "assume you don't know" fall within a type of leadership ideology I call benevolent accountability with pragmatic creativity. This ideology mixes two complementary philosophies.

Another example of an organization that has crafted meaningful corporate values to guide leadership ideology is DaVita Kidney Care. A longtime client of mine, DaVita provides valuable renal care around the world. The source of their benevolent accountability approach resides – quite literally – in "The Village," which is DaVita's term to describe their culture. The DaVita Way includes commitment to a set of corporate values. These values are less conceptual than most: service excellence, integrity, team, continuous improvement, accountability, fulfillment, and fun – but still a bit soft. There are several reasons why these expressed values have more impact than the usual poster-on-the-wall experience. For one, each team member, or "citizen" (the term used to describe members of the DaVita village), attends training on the corporate culture. At the culmination of the meeting, villagers are invited to cross a bridge – yes, an actual bridge – on stage to represent their commitment to the DaVita way. While that ceremony may bring out some rolling eyes, I saw the impact firsthand.

As a frequent vendor/partner, I was invited to become an honorary villager. The training sessions are extremely high energy, steeped in solid training techniques, and, most importantly, contain a great deal of audience participation that reinforces the behaviors expected to match the values. At every single meeting where I presented to a DaVita audience – and we are talking dozens and dozens across the United States – the corporate values were on display and the language of the DaVita Way was used. The impact of this culture even influenced my presentations. I took great care to draw a link between my content and their core values by starting each seminar by pointing out that this experience relates to service excellence, team, continuous improvement, and fun. Imagine a corporate culture within which every meeting was expressly connected to the values of the organization. That is what DaVita accomplished. As a result, the beliefs of leadership were instilled at all levels of the organization. In fact, the values DaVita expresses as core to their success were identified and agreed to by the employee base – not by leadership.

That's another key to the success of good corporate values. One absolute truth of organizations is that there are always more non-leaders than leaders. Reconciling that imbalance of perspective is vital to a peak performance culture.

Benevolent accountability is a leadership ideology based on several ingredients all designed to achieve high levels of performance while simultaneously being mindful of the inherent needs of the individuals you lead. People have lives, and those lives are complicated. To pretend that the human beings who populate the organization can compartmentalize their lives in such an absolute way as not to allow any part of their personal life to affect their job is not reasonable. Great organizations balance an assertive commitment to peak performance with a sensitivity to the complexities of the forces present in each employee's life. After all, an organization is simply a collection of people. To pretend that we can lead an organization without being mindful of the needs of the individual people makes no sense at all – unless you plan to populate your company with robots.

Benevolent accountability starts with the belief that all employees want to be successful. Is this true? Perhaps not, but I feel strongly that believing otherwise will only lead to cynicism and negativity. It is far better to believe in the best of others and be disappointed occasionally than to be suspicious of others and be proven right – particularly since the latter mindset in a leader can create a self-fulfilling prophecy. Besides, who wants to live in a world where people aspire only to mediocrity? Not me.

Pragmatic creativity represents the other important mindset of peak performance leadership and reconciles a common challenge for organizations: the origin of innovation. Many – in fact, most – of my clients over the years boast of a visionary approach to their operation. They maintain that someone – the founder, owner, CEO, or the like – has identified a unique future state for the organization that guides their successful efforts and distinguishes them from their competitors. I don't disagree with the importance of brand differentiators to organizational success, as made evident by the chapter on Horizontal Alignment. However, finding true visionary leaders like Jobs, Bezos, Gates, or Walton – well, good luck. The truth is that most organizations are led by energetic, intelligent individuals who use passion, effort, research, and commitment rather than a savant with unrivaled abilities to imagine the future. Pragmatic creativity doesn't require the practitioner to conjure up a unique future state. This form of creativity is based on maintaining an openness to change and implementing it with structure, tactics, and facts. Creative and pragmatic.

Some people can pull creativity out of thin air. They are organizational artists, able to work with a blank canvas to create a desired future state. Listening to them talk about the desired future state is like watching a talented artist paint. They have a keen mental image of the final version of the work, but the observer sees only a white space that slowly takes form. For the observer, the painting must be near completion before it becomes recognizable. For the artist, it was always recognizable – even when there was nothing on the canvas. These "artists" are rare in organizations. More commonly, great leaders are problem solvers who continually look for opportunities to improve the organization with better ideas combined with clear strategies for realizing them. They do their work after the image has taken shape. That is pragmatic creativity.

The bottom line is that few organizations build a culture out of a unique, creative expression of conceptual ideals or novel approaches. Most peak performance cultures enlist a more practical approach. They build their organization around leadership principles that transcend subjective interpretation. They identify techniques that can be specifically defined, identified in others at the time of employee selection, taught to those who do not currently possess them, and measured for ongoing impact. Rather than focus on corporate values, these organizations focus on leadership ideology – which comprises both methodology and mentality. It is an orientation to leading that provides a map for peak performance. More specifically, a leadership ideology that reflects benevolent accountability and pragmatic creativity is critical to peak performance cultures. This ideology starts with a concept that I address in every book I write: internal locus of control.

INTERNAL LOCUS OF CONTROL

For those of you who have read each of my previous three books, thank you! Also, I am keenly aware that I continually hammer on this quality of internal locus of control. I do so because I believe it to be the single most important personal characteristic to success and happiness in life. If you are not familiar with the term, here's how I explain it.

Imagine that life is like beef stew. As you progress through life, you will experience times that are easy – like you are moving through the broth. Much of the time we are unaware we are moving through the broth because things are progressing as we expect them to. We live our normal days, going through the routines that populate our day. Then, often without warning, you hit a carrot or an onion or a piece of beef. These represent the unforeseen developments in your life – often negative – that can redirect your journey away from your planned path. Stew contains carrots and onions and beef, so it should come as no surprise that a journey through it would likely include running into those ingredients. When the inevitable occurs, we face some choices. Some people will blame the carrot, lamenting the impact of this unexpected development on their life. They consider the broth to be their permanent state and the contact with the carrot is an unwelcome – and unwarranted – exception. This is an *external* locus of control. This person believes – consciously or subconsciously – that they are entitled to a carrot-free life. This expectation is rationally flawed, so the behaviors of the external locus of control-oriented person betray reason. "Why did this happen to me? I can't believe I have to deal with a carrot!" Of course, you do, because carrots are part of stew (life).

Others will immediately look inward to determine what they need to do to return to their planned path after having hit the carrot. Even better, they may have anticipated the collision with the carrot and already have contingency for this potentiality. They recognize that life, like stew, contains many elements. Some will be amazing, most will be mundane, and some will be difficult. Life is also random. Some spoonfuls contain carrots, others onions, some both, some neither, and so on. Life just happens, but *your* life is your responsibility. That is an internal locus of control. To paraphrase the stuff of motivational posters: life isn't what happens to you; it's what you do after it happens.

Basically, there are two reactions to life's challenges: taking responsibility for them or blaming something or someone else. While not all the negative developments in our life are our fault, we are the only person accountable for our own life. It does us no good to allow ourselves to be the victim of life developments. As part of a leadership ideology, an internal locus of control encourages individuals to act to move situations toward successful outcomes. For example, here are some questions that great leaders may ask themselves to reinforce an internal locus of control when faced with a challenge or unhappy customer:

- What can I do to create a positive experience for this customer?
- What do I need to do in the future to avoid this mistake?
- How can I impact this process to improve it?
- What can I do to enhance the teamwork within the organization?
- What can I do to improve the team's performance?
- What can I learn from this mistake?

Notice a pattern in these questions? Each one involves reflecting on one's *own influence* over the situation. Good leaders not only ask themselves these kinds of questions; they also facilitate that same introspection with the teams they lead. Steve Thompson at PrimeLending goes so far as to ask his direct reports to complete a "Dos and Don'ts of Communicating with You." He uses these guidelines to ensure that he isn't making mistakes in his leadership style. He also revisits this list from time to time with his team members to make sure he is being consistent with their expectations. In this way, he is displaying an internal locus of control for the effectiveness of his relationship with his direct reports. Many leaders put the ownership on the team when it comes to communication with them – a behavior that reflects an external locus of control.

One final consideration as it relates to an internal locus of control. Failure is one of the most important leadership development tools. In the 25 years of the Leadership Difference, Inc., I have had many more good years than tough years. In fact, from 1995 to 2007, the company grew substantially every year. It is easy to take full credit for that success, but the fact is success is an equation that combines good practices with luck. The problem is knowing the role of luck. When the economy slumped wildly in 2008, I knew exactly how much luck had contributed to my previous success. That's the profundity of failure. It reveals the impact of luck and reminds you of your own limitations. The experience of surviving 2008–2011 during one of the most challenging global economies of my lifetime made me a far better leader. It also reinforced the importance of an internal locus of control as it required that I take responsibility for determining a path forward. I know of others who were content to blame the economy and give up on their visions. Many companies disappeared in those 3–4 years.

An internal locus of control that is prevalent throughout the organization provides the foundation for reconciling one of the biggest challenges within an organization: influence versus impact.

AN EMPOWERMENT CULTURE

Organizational executive leadership wields incredible influence. Decisions about products, services, goals, strategies, and methodology are made every day in boardrooms around the world. When done thoughtfully, these decisions are designed to guide the organization toward successful horizontal and vertical alignment. Executives have abundant influence. Conversely, they do not have much impact. That is why ego can be a destructive element to successful leadership ideology. Executives who overvalue their impact fundamentally misunderstand their role in the company. An organization's impact rests in the execution of the employees who are either in direct contact with the customer or in direct contact with an employee who is (the internal customer). Executives have influence but little impact; employees have impact but little influence. In between are mid-level leaders – managers, supervisors, leads – who are trying to ensure the implementation of the influence through the execution of the impact. It is a critical fulcrum of organizational excellence. The most meaningful employee coaching falls to this level. This is the group that can practice benevolent accountability. It is also the most often overlooked level.

My experience has been that training resources are more generously allotted for employee skill training and executive development. Both are important, for sure. Unfortunately, the one population that represents the focal point between influence and impact – middle management – is often given short shrift when it comes to professional development. Many of the individuals in this group were never given leadership training, have often been promoted based on skills unrelated to leadership abilities, and lack the confidence required to navigate the role in which they find themselves. If a company's success revolves around executing on a clear vision, it is this level of leadership that connects the concept with the pragmatic. Executives envision; employees execute. Between them are the critical contributors who must interpret the strategy and ensure it gets applied.

These are the individuals who vertically align the organization. If this is not done effectively, the best visions go unfulfilled. Ultimately, no executive or employee alone can compel their organization to sustainable success.

An empowerment culture's hallmark is the elevation of middle management's importance. Positioned between executives and employees, middle management is the toughest of all jobs in the organization. Grievances, criticisms, and continuous negative feedback can come from both directions. An incompetent executive can be protected by exceptional managers. An incompetent employee can be covered by an exceptional manager. Neither of these are optimal, nor are they uncommon. But an incompetent manager will damage the performance of several employees and can bring down the efforts of the best executives.

My first significant client project after starting the Leadership Difference, Inc. in 1995 was developing the Certified Leader Program for Rosen Hotels and Resorts (called Tamar Inns back in those days). The goal was to build upon their management training – a curriculum that was largely based on procedural training. Harris Rosen, the legendary central Florida hotelier and namesake of the organization, was an influential supporter of education and imagined this program to be a sort of graduate degree in leadership for new leaders. I constructed classes delivered monthly over the course of a year that covered topics like motivation, law, interviewing, coaching, counseling, performance feedback, customer service, conflict resolution, and employee training. Each class included homework that required the participants to apply what they had learned and write reflection papers on their efforts. We even conducted a study under the direction of the University of Illinois at Urbana–Champaign to determine the impact of the course.

Statistical analysis validated that graduates of the Rosen Hotels and Resorts Certified Leader Program experienced a measurable increase in skills self-efficacy as a result of the curriculum. Self-efficacy is an underappreciated contributor to peak performance and one that I examine in detail in Chapter 6, "The Employee Experience." In short, attending this program increased the new managers' confidence in each of the skills addressed in the classes.

Confidence, combined with competency, is a key to peak performance execution. During the twenty years that I facilitated this program, I watched leaders progress through the company, witnessed the organization's continued success and growth, and developed relationships that continue today. Those are the hallmarks of an empowerment culture.

Preparing midlevel leaders *before* they are promoted into this role reflects a commitment to operational excellence. Many of the best organizations prepare succession plans to respond to the sudden departure/promotion of individuals. Taking that a step further, the peak performance culture would invest time and resources preparing those team members on succession plans for their eventual leadership role. Inviting them to participate in management training is one strategy. At the Buena Vista Palace Resort and Spa in Orlando, Florida, we utilized another.

In 1992, the total quality management (TQM) approach to leadership was not common within the hospitality industry. TQM was far more popular among manufacturing companies. That began to change largely due to the efforts of Horst Schulze at the Ritz-Carlton Hotel Company. That year, Ritz-Carlton won the prestigious Malcolm Baldrige National Quality Award. I remember this distinctly because we were also competing for this award. I remain bitter. Kidding. (Kinda.)

Anyway, our own efforts to integrate a TQM approach to hotel management included an element designed to prepare our next middle managers for their inevitable leadership role. Like many high-performing organizations, we had a group of impressive employees who were ready for more responsibility but were forced to wait for an opening. These were role models of peak performance who were eager for the next challenge. We didn't want to lose them, so to satisfy their ambition and prepare them for their future leadership role, we created a new role: Red Coats.

As the name suggests, Red Coats were given a red coat to wear at work. Their primary jobs were in specific departments, but their red coat role spanned the entire hotel. The purpose of the coat was to draw attention to them among both customers and employees. We encouraged the Red Coats to respond to and resolve customer and employee questions, regardless of whether it was within their job responsibilities. They were empowered to cross organizational boundaries (more on the concept of seam-work later) to improve operational efficiency, satisfy customers and employees, and serve as a vivid example of performance excellence. Red Coats met once each month to share data they had collected from customers and employees and discuss ways to improve the hotel. It was not just a leadership preparation strategy; it also helped to reconcile the authority/impact imbalance in the organization.

The peak performance culture will place a high value on management and leadership development for those vital roles between executives and employees. Decisions to promote individuals to this level will be thoughtful. Great care will be taken to support their dual challenge of understanding the long-term, big-picture view of the organization while also ensuring that products and services are delivered each day that reflect the quality required to please the customer. This is the essence of pragmatic creativity. An empowerment culture, one that develops the abilities of mid-level managers, is a critical component to a benevolent accountability and pragmatic creativity approach to leadership ideology.

INTRINSIC NEEDS FULFILLMENT

The importance of a leadership ideology predicated on benevolent accountability is never more obvious than its impact on the intrinsic needs of the organization's employees. As I have discussed in my last two books, individuals perform at their highest capabilities when their respective intrinsic needs are being met within the organizational environment. There are four iconic intrinsic needs that we all possess. While each of us desire all four, we have a primary intrinsic need based on our preferred interactive style.

Some employees – individuals I call "Romantics" – thrive in workplaces that contain abundant praise and appreciation. These employees often self-sacrifice, take on job responsibilities that others avoid, and volunteer to do tasks when others refuse. In exchange for being eager team players, they desire the recognition of their leader – even if they outwardly express no need for such. These contributors are emotionally sensitive and seek to know that their leader genuinely recognizes their dedication and loyalty. A leader who practices a "no news is good news" approach to employee communication will demotivate this employee.

As previously described, "Warriors" get things done. They are typically efficient performers and highly productive. They prefer a leader who provides direction and then leaves them alone to accomplish the desired outcome. Independence is the intrinsic reward that drives their performance. Their logical orientation contributes to a keen awareness and disdain for activities, interactions, and processes that are unnecessary. Competitive and renowned for being a self-starter, this type of employee finds a meddlesome leader to be a nightmare.

If Warriors are known for the quantity of their work, "Experts" are the quality contributors. They apply best practices based on their personal experiences. They rue mistakes, particularly ones that they have made, and strive to avoid them at all costs. Being accurate – doing things the right way – requires depth of information. They are most comfortable in situations that provide comprehensive training and education, consistent policies and procedures, and few surprises. Romantics soar with praise, Warriors with independence, and the Experts with security.

Finally, "Masterminds" are the risk takers. They have an entrepreneurial orientation. The thought of repetitive, predictable routines does not inspire them and, in fact, bores them. Masterminds like what's new and different and will seek novel challenges, special projects, and other ways to customize their employment experience. They need options. Leading a Mastermind requires that you continually stimulate them with new directions, responsibilities, and possibilities.

The terms "benevolent accountability" and "pragmatic creativity" in many ways reflect the four types of interactive style and their respective intrinsic needs: benevolent (Romantic), accountability (Warrior), pragmatic (Expert), and creativity (Mastermind). Any effective leadership ideology must be inclusive of and accessible to all styles. Fulfilling these four intrinsic needs – appreciation, independence, security, and options – assures that your leadership ideology is contributing to peak performance. For more information on the four iconic styles of people, check out my book *The Power of Understanding People*.

DIALECTICAL THINKING

"Internal locus of control" is easily the first characteristic uttered from my lips when people ask me about peak performance culture. Right behind it is dialectical thinking. At first glance, the idea that dialectical thinking even needs to be emphasized as a component of high-performance culture seems silly. Like honesty, care, and integrity, dialectical thinking should be a no-brainer in creating the foundation of behaviors in any organization. Sadly, this is far from true. Let's begin with defining the term as it applies to my purposes, then examine why this obviously critical element of culture is far too rare within organizations.

When evaluating an organization's culture, I have found that evidence of a dialectical style of leadership is conducive to peak performance. Unlike the other philosophies for resolving conflicting opinions, the basis of dialectical thinking is initiating a dialogue with others to determine the truth.

What do I mean by dialectical thinking? Let me offer a story. Imagine two people – let's say Bob and Jack – having a nice glass of wine and discussing the news of the day. I would picture this happening at a lovely wine bar with comfy seats and a view of a bustling street just outside. It's a sunny day, not too warm. The wine is a French rosé. (Too much detail?) So, we have two people having a conversation about current events. As they sip their wine, a homeless person walks by them on the sidewalk outside the bar. Bob says to Jack, "It is so sad that a nation as prosperous as ours has people who do not have a place to live."

Jack responds, "*Meh*, there are plenty of jobs and support available. If that person really wanted to get off the street, they would seek out that support, get a job, and rent a place to live. My bet is that they prefer to beg for drug money and live the way they are."

"So, you think someone *wants* to live like that?" Bob can barely conceal his irritation.

"I'm just saying they have a choice. If they want to get off the street, they can. They choose not to. I know this to be true because we have hired homeless people to do odd jobs at my workplace and they show up one time, get some cash, and never come back."

Not content with this response, Bob fires back, "You don't know the details of their life. Maybe they have a medical problem. It could be addiction, or it could be a mental illness or some other problem that keeps them from being able to work. To just dismiss their situation as a lack of initiative is to have no compassion for their situation."

"No compassion for their situation!" Jack is becoming angry at the insinuation that he is not a good person. "I volunteer at a homeless shelter through my church. I give money. I want these people off the streets and leading productive lives. We all benefit, them and us, if they contribute to our society in a positive way. Allowing them a free ride to just take handouts, live on the street, and make our parks and neighborhood look like shit when there is an entire infrastructure of support for them not two blocks away is not being cold hearted. I work. I contribute to society. Excuse me if I don't think they should just panhandle, drink, and do drugs and expect me to pay for it. Look, I get that people have mental health problems or addictions or whatever, but there are many resources to help these people. If they want to make their situation better, they can. Many of them don't."

Bob's voice is starting to rise. "So, you think many of these people are just lazy freeloaders who enjoy sleeping in a box under the overpass? Many of the homeless are military veterans. Were they lazy freeloaders when they served our country? That's bullshit, Jack."

"Whatever, Bob. That's not what I said." Jack turns to the server who is passing by. "Check, please."

It is unlikely that either Bob or Jack has changed their position on homelessness. The point of the story is not who is right or wrong; the point is that the relationship between Bob and Jack may have been negatively affected by the way that they discussed the issue. This effect may be only momentary, it may linger for days or weeks, or it could last forever. Regardless of the duration, the effect is toxic. Further, neither Bob nor Jack likely changed their opinion on the issue one bit. In fact, it likely pushed them further into their own perspective while creating an antagonism in their relationship.

Now, let's revisit the same conversation using a dialectical thinking approach. The wine bar setting and the French rosé remain the same.

Bob observes, "It is so sad that a nation as prosperous as ours has people who do not have a place to live."

Jack responds, "I don't think it's related to the nation's prosperity. I think there are ample resources and jobs available for the homeless if they choose to take advantage of them. I think they choose to live on the street because it is easier than working or finding support."

"That's interesting." Bob probes further. "What about individuals with mental health issues, addictions, or who just simply do not have the means to get to work? I think there are many legitimate barriers prohibiting homeless people from changing their circumstances even with jobs and resources available."

"Perhaps. What I know is that many of the homeless people we have hired for odd jobs at my work never come back once they get some cash. I also know, through the work at my church, that they can get support for food, shelter, and clothing. It just seems to me that if they want to get back on their feet, they could."

Bob nods. "The work you are doing at your church and the support of your workplace are fantastic. It could well be that some people abuse these resources. I also think there are many people who face very difficult circumstances that have made it almost impossible for them to escape homelessness. Mental health care can be difficult to access and maintain. Did you know that many homeless people are military veterans?"

Jack nods. "Yeah, I have heard that. That is really sad. We should do a much better job caring for our veterans. I think we probably need to do a better job at outreach to get these folks the help they need so they can contribute more to society."

"Agreed. I am sure there are some people who choose to be homeless. I just think that we can do a better job as a nation helping those who haven't made that choice."

"Yep."

The two conversations are essentially the same, with one very important distinguishing characteristic – the second example utilized dialectic thinking to discuss the differences in the perspectives of the two men. In the first example, the two men engaged in an argument over who was right. Depending on your own point of view, you may have aligned more with one or the other. In their respective efforts to change the mind of the other person, they became increasingly more entrenched in their own point of view. Bob and Jack listened for areas of disagreement that they could attack as wrong. Their debate was based on an antagonistic dialogue. The resultant conflict was a predictable outcome for this approach.

In the second example, each person expressed their current perspective. When they listened to each other's point of view, they looked for areas of agreement rather than conflict. In this way, their debate was based on respect. When you debate an issue respectfully, you are not engaged in argument but rather exploration. Bob and Jack are considering a broader understanding of the topic. Dialectical thinking is about using two perspectives to arrive at a third, more robust perspective. In my definition, a dialectical approach requires you to assume that just as you arrived at your opinion in a reasoned, rational way, so did those whose perspective differs from yours. As a result, we both have things to learn from each other and the greater truth will emerge from that dialogue.

There are essentially three ways to approach a disagreement: universalistic, relativistic, or dialectic. Universalistic thinking means that there is a single, correct perspective on the issue. This means that in every argument someone is right and someone is wrong. Unfortunately, this doesn't encourage dialogue since the person who is made to feel wrong will likely find another argument to get even. Think about it: Have you ever really "won" an argument with your spouse or significant other? More likely, you just extended the single issue into a best of three series of arguments. It's conflict resolution executed like an NBA playoff round.

Relativistic thinking reflects the whole, a "different strokes for different folks" way of resolving differences. The belief of relativists is – well, it's relative. I feel the way I feel based on the context of my life while you feel differently because of the context of your life. "You do you," as people are fond of saying these days. The problem with this approach is there is no need for dialogue because no one need change their perspective anyway. It is essentially "agreeing to disagree."

In a peak performance organization – one that manifests benevolent accountability and pragmatic creativity – the culture must be open to reconciling differences using respectful dialogue that generates broader and better resolutions. Dialectical thinking requires the following:

- Mutual respect for another's perspective especially when it is different from your own
- The freedom to express your point of view
- Listening to other perspectives to find areas of agreement, which requires a genuine interest in hearing a point of view that differs from your own
- An eagerness to expand and enhance your perspective

One final note on dialectical thinking: dialectics is a way of discussing issues that have no specific moral correctness. There are clearly some issues that are black and white as it relates to workplace conduct. Harassment, theft, lying, and unlawfulness are all areas that are not subjected to dialectical thinking because they are non-starters. Dialectical thinking is less a value and more a philosophy or methodology in this application. With that said, the peak performance culture has a successful conflict resolution process and a dialectical approach that works well. Imagine an organization where people are respected for their perspectives, are free to share them, and resolve differences by finding areas of agreement that lead to broader and better new perspectives. Pretty cool, huh?

ZERO-BASED THINKING

There is an undeniably uncomfortable moment during every one of my keynote speeches on leadership ideology. Here's when it happens:

"I need everyone to close their eyes right now."

Yes, that seems like this would be the uncomfortable moment – when the keynote speaker asks a few hundred people in a conference center in Las Vegas to close their eyes. That's not the moment I am referring to. Stay with me.

"I want you to picture all the individuals on your team – all the employees who look to you for leadership. Line them up in your mind's eye along a wall and walk down that line looking each of them in the face."

"Now, ask yourself this question, 'Knowing what I know about your performance now, would I hire you again?'"

"Keep your eyes closed. Raise your hands if you answered that question with a 'no' about any of your current team."

Then comes the uncomfortable moment for me. That's because nearly every leader in that meeting room raises their hand. Nearly every leader admits that they have at least one member on their team whom they would not hire again if given the opportunity.

Next comes the uncomfortable moment for them.

"Open your eyes. It is my duty to inform you that nearly every one of you raised your hand. That tells me that nearly every one of you has someone on your staff who is not performing at a level that you expect. That means you have at least one person who is below your expectation of what is satisfactory. So, my next question is, what are you doing about it? If your answer is 'nothing,' then *you* are the problem."

Benevolent accountability in leadership begins as an adherence to a personal standard. Leaders must ask themselves, "Am I doing what is necessary to ensure peak performance in this organization?" It is easy to slough off on one or two team members whose performance is less than remarkable. It seems like an innocuous decision to allow underperformers – particularly those who are otherwise not toxic and maintain a positive attitude – to continue to generate substandard work. Unfortunately, the decision to tolerate substandard work does not exist in a vacuum.

The literal definition of a performance standard is the minimum level of quality and quantity at which a task must be completed to satisfy the requirements of the job. The evaluator of this level of quality and quantity is the leader. If the leader accepts a level of quality and quantity generated by a team member and maintains their employment, then that performer has met the standard. It does not matter what level of performance is stated or expected, only what is accepted.

As a result, when the leader accepts a level of quality and quantity below the stated expectation, that leader has now lowered the standard. When a leader lowers the standard, the impact of that decision is not limited to the performer responsible for the work product that is below the stated expectation. Other performers attenuate their efforts and work product relative to their perception of the standard. If the standard is lowered, then they lower their quality and quantity. This does not just apply to team members who perform at the expected standard, but also to those who are performing above standard. Team members who perform at high levels do so relative to the expected standard. So, if a leader reduces the standard, they also reduce the performance of high performers relative to that standard.

The metaphor is like measuring the height of boats in a harbor. Let's say the tallest boat is 6 feet taller than the next tallest boat, 15 feet higher than the shortest boat, and 20 feet higher than the water. If the water goes down, the tallest boat is still taller than the next tallest, the shortest, and the water by the same amount. However, all the boats are now shorter because the depth of the water has fallen. In this way, the water is like the standard. When you drop the expected standard, the performance of all team members goes down.

When a leader engages in zero-based thinking – and they should with frequency – it is completely acceptable to identify performers who are not meeting expectations. The term "zero-based" refers to a return to the zero point of a decision, that point when the decision was made. So, engaging in zero-based thinking literally means returning to that moment but now with the advantage of additional data. That is the value of this element of peak performance culture – to identify areas where improvements are necessary by reevaluating decisions with updated data. Great leaders make mistakes and poor decisions on occasion. They sometimes hire the wrong person for a job. However, if the leader is not engaging in some process of coaching and/or counseling to improve that team member's performance, the exercise should now be uncomfortable. Benevolent accountability and pragmatic creativity involve doing what is necessary to shift peak performance responsibility from the leader to the team member.

COACHING AND COUNSELING TO SHIFT RESPONSIBILITY

I spent a dozen years in corporate human resources development. This period was split evenly between positions specializing in training and development and generalist functions in human resources management. When I was a human resources generalist, a significant part of my responsibility was consulting with leaders to review and approve their approach to addressing employee performance, particularly performance that was deemed to be below our standards. It was in this capacity that I became aware of a significant deficiency among many leaders that I found alarming – and that is that many leaders did not feel accountable for their own team members' failures.

It seems obvious to me – and it has been my experience in the classroom that others agree – that when a person is considered the leader of a team, they are assumed to be ultimately responsible for the performance of that team. In sports, the first person who will likely lose their job if a team underperforms is the coach. In this case, sports is a good metaphor for all organizations. Poor leaders create poor teams. You can imagine how I responded to the following common scenario:

"Hey, Dave, do you have a minute?"

"Of course, Mateo, what's up?"

"I wanted to talk to you about Jed. He's a problem. I just don't think he's a good fit for our department."

"Jed? He's new, right?"

"Well, he's been here almost six months, so he's not that new."

"Okay. Let me pull his 90-day review."

This was often an uncomfortable development for the leader. I was always surprised that someone would want to discuss the performance of an employee without me looking at what was in their human resources file. It was the first mental alarm bell for me.

"Mateo, you wrote his 90-day review and listed his work as 'exceeding expectations.' Has his performance decreased since then?"

"I was probably being generous. We were shorthanded, so I didn't want to lose him, plus I know he needs money, so I wanted him to get a good merit increase at 90 days."

While I might commend Mateo for his honesty, all I could think of was that two of our gross misconduct provisions – situations that resulted in immediate termination – were falsifying a company document and theft. At this point it sounded like we should be firing Mateo rather than Jed.

"So, you are telling me that you have had concerns about Jed since he was hired six months ago?"

"Yep, pretty much."

"Well, Mateo, I have some bad news. I don't think the problem is Jed right now. I think the problem is you."

It was clear from Mateo's nonverbal behavioral cues that this was *not* how he imagined this conversation going down. Mateo had failed to understand that Jed's performance was *his* responsibility. If Jed was performing below expectation, Mateo had a duty to do what was necessary to fix that. This includes:

- Effectively communicate the job responsibilities and the required standard to which they are to be performing.
- Provide training on each of these job responsibilities.
- Provide continuous feedback – both affirmative and critical – on the performance of responsibilities.
- Shift responsibility for meeting standards from the leader to the team member.

I have often heard that when an employee is not meeting performance standards, it's because they are either unwilling or unable. My experience is that the far more common reason is a third scenario: they are unaware. Regardless of which reason – unwillingness, inability, or lack of awareness – the same process can be used to address the challenge. It begins with the leader assuming accountability for the problem.

In a traditional model for employee coaching and counseling – often referred to as "progressive discipline" – there are four steps:

- Verbal warning
- Written warning
- Final warning or suspension
- Termination

In a peak performance culture, these four steps are executed by the leader using this approach:

- My fault
- Our fault
- Your fault
- Termination

There is a huge difference in the efficacy of verbal warnings that are conducted with a tone that indicates that the reason for the team member's performance deficiency is due to the leader's lack of effectively communicating expectations or providing sufficient training. Imagine being Jed and consider which of these two approaches to performance counseling would likely be more effective when executed by Mateo.

"Jed, I am very concerned about your performance. You are not meeting our expected standards. If you continue to perform at this level, you could eventually lose your job. I am going to need you to improve your performance."

Or:

"Jed, I believe I have failed to communicate my expectations for the performance of your responsibilities. Let's discuss the standards for each of your job duties. As we do, please let me know what I can provide you in regard to training and resources to execute at that level."

While neither of these conversations will be fun, the latter approach is far less confrontational and is a better reflection of a leader who has taken responsibility for the team member's performance. It also eliminates one of the three possible reasons for Jed's performance situation: lack of awareness. Jed's performance may improve simply because he now clearly understands what is expected. Furthermore, based on Jed's response, Mateo may discover the competency gap between Jed's current ability and what is necessary to meet the standards. This revelation will lead to additional training to fix Jed's inability – the second of the three reasons for a performance deficiency. Through training, Mateo will learn if Jed ultimately can do the job.

If the initial verbal warning – the "my fault" leader conversation – fails to adequately improve Jed's performance, then the responsibility becomes shared. A written warning reflects that a problem is now being shifted from the leader's responsibility to that of both parties. It sounds something like this:

"Jed, last month we discussed the need to increase your performance level to meet the organizational standards. I feel like I clearly communicated those expectations and I offered the support of additional training or other resources if you needed them. Unfortunately, your performance is still not meeting standards. I want you to be successful. If there is something you do not understand about our performance standards or how to achieve them, please let me know. Continued performance at this level is not acceptable and could result in your termination."

If there was a chance that the first conversation failed to resolve a lack of awareness or ability, this step will likely correct that failure. The clear implication is that the current state of performance is untenable and that something will change, either the employee's performance or their employment status. It has been my experience that any change in employee behavior and performance is most likely to occur after the verbal or written warning because it is during these steps that a lack of awareness or ability are ferreted out. If a team member is unable to do the job, they most likely will admit that during this stage. If Jed is unwilling, he may continue to perform below standard even with the knowledge that the situation will eventually be addressed by the leader.

By the time of the final warning or suspension, the accountability for the performance deficiency has now shifted entirely from the leader to the team member. At this point, the organization/Mateo is essentially doing a reverse two weeks' notice to Jed in that he is letting him know that unless an unexpected improvement occurs in his performance, he will lose his job. The hope is that Jed uses this period to find a position in which he is willing and able to meet the standard. The best possible outcome is an amicable parting of the ways.

In a peak performance culture, leaders take full responsibility for their team members' performance. When performance deficiencies are identified, the leader assumes this situation reflects a lack of awareness or training, both of which are the accountability of the leader. When continued efforts to educate and train the team member fail to improve the team member's performance, the accountability for their performance shifts to them. The resulting process results in substandard performers self-selecting out of the organization.

Benevolent accountability and pragmatic creativity are not limited to addressing performance deficiencies. Quite the contrary. Exceptional leadership ideology focuses on those who exceed performance standards. One of the most common failures of leadership is the tendency to take peak performance for granted – the whole "no news is good news" approach to leading performance. The peak performance culture must have a mechanism for continually monitoring and recognizing *high* performance as well.

PEOPLE PREVENTATIVE MAINTENANCE SYSTEM

I think all professionals, over the course of their career and regardless of the discipline, will discover widely accepted practices that they don't support. For me, there are two classic tools used by human resources professionals that I think are not only ineffective but I actually believe do more harm than good. One is the employee recognition program – the employee of the month, quarter, year, whatever. The traditional example is to gather the organization together each month and present a plaque and a convenient parking spot to the single most valuable employee.

My problem with these programs is that, at best, they are appealing to a small percentage of the employee base while potentially alienating the vast majority. That seems mighty counterproductive to the purpose of the program. A plaque and parking spot don't really capture any employee's fundamental needs. Referring to my interactive style descriptors, Romantics want to be appreciated. While an employee of the month award would appear to accomplish that on the surface, the reality is that Romantics can feel uncomfortable with being publicly honored; it places them on a pedestal above their peers and risks their relationships with co-workers. They prefer a more personal affirmation of gratitude. Romantics may conspire to rotate the award so that no one feels left out or elevated above the rest of the team. The Warriors don't need to be told they are the best; they already know, and would prefer a cash award since that has a great deal more value than a plaque. Experts are likely to impeach the selection criterion, thus invalidating the award winner, and Masterminds likely have no idea the program even exists. For me, employee recognition programs as I have described them are a waste of money, effort, and time.

My other pet peeve in human resources management is the employee opinion survey. This may seem contradictory to my views stated on horizontal alignment that include the need to achieve employee satisfaction. Theoretically, an incredibly well-designed data collection process combined with effective post-survey feedback could be a great system for monitoring and enhancing employee satisfaction. The problem for me is that I have yet to see this system used. Mostly, what I have seen is an annual exercise in requiring employees to answer questions about the work experience using a Likert scale (four or five potential responses ranging from awful to great) with some room for providing a more expansive response via comments. The resulting data will likely confirm the following:

- The organization does not pay well enough.
- The organization should add or improve the benefits package.
- There is at least one team member in each department who is very critical of their leader.
- Overall, people are satisfied with their jobs.
- The organization doesn't really know much more about the employee perspective after this massive undertaking than it did before it, but the whole thing took a lot of everyone's time.

Further aggravating the situation is that upon completion of this endeavor, the organization will:

- Not increase pay
- Make few or no changes in the benefits package
- Do nothing with the feedback about the leader
- Not discuss the results with the employees since not much was really learned
- Vow to repeat this exercise next year

For those readers who have managed to avoid these pitfalls and install an effective employee opinion process, good on ya!

But my experience is that many organizations haven't. In fact, most of the companies that choose to do employee opinion surveys are doing more harm to their organizational health by doing so. The ceremony of collecting employee data only to discover little and/or do nothing with this information is soul crushing to all involved. The intentions are good, but the execution is not.

A far better approach to collecting feedback relative to employee satisfaction is to use a more casual mechanism. I have found that effective leaders seek feedback frequently by allowing employees the space to share their frustrations, excitement, and ideas. I dubbed this process the "People Preventative Maintenance System." (In *The Power of Understanding People*, I referred to this system on pages 133–34.) It's a simple system that works like this:

- Create a spreadsheet with all your team members' names in the left column and the months of the year as headers for the next 12 columns:

Team Member	Jan	Feb	Mar	Apr	May	June	July	Aug	Sept	Oct	Nov	Dec
Sally												
Ahmad												
Pietra												
Bill												

- Each month, schedule a casual 15-minute meeting with each of your team members. The key is to execute the meeting informally but track it formally to ensure that you speak with each team member each month. For example, you may conduct the meeting while grabbing a cup of coffee or taking a brief walk so that it feels spontaneous; but you should note the meeting on your spreadsheet so that you ensure you have conducted PPM meetings with each team member.

- Ask the team member the following questions (or similar ones that feel more natural to you). Each of these questions may open additional areas for discussion, so while the meetings generally last only 15 minutes, you may want to schedule 30 minutes on your calendar to avoid feeling rushed.
  - How are things going at work?
  - What do you like most?
  - What do you like least?
  - What would you change in the department to improve our work?
  - What do you need to make it easier for you to be successful?
  - How can I better support you?
- Have a conversation about the answers. Some of the team members' ideas may include suggestions that you will be unable to make happen. If so, discuss this with the team member so that they understand why you can't institute change.
- Make notes on the feedback – particularly on team member suggestions that you can and should implement. Determine what must be done, research their practicality, and respond to the team member within a few days about the status of their suggestion.
- PPM systems often take several months to truly hit their stride. During the initial months, team members may be reticent to share their honest feedback or suspicious that any changes will result. Once you have asked for their input several times and they have seen their ideas implemented, team members will be more eager to participate and share.

The key to a successful People Preventative Maintenance System is that you are consistent in collecting the information and reliable in acting on what you collect. This cycle creates an internal continuous improvement process based on employee feedback, which in turn helps assure high levels of employee satisfaction and reflects benevolent accountability and pragmatic creativity.

SEAMWORK

That's not a typo. *Seamwork* is a word I use to describe the interdepartmental relationships within an organization. Traditionally, companies pay a great deal of attention to teamwork within functional units. I have done many team building programs for sales teams, customer service representatives, and leadership teams. Far fewer clients have hired me to strengthen the communication and collaboration between functional teams. However, as it relates to peak performance, it is these very relationships that signal a high level of function and vertical alignment.

The classic dysfunctional seam in many companies is between business development and service delivery – sales versus operations. The nature of their jobs fundamentally creates friction. I know this not just from the work with my clients but also from firsthand knowledge. In my company, I almost always identify, develop, and close client business. I am also the primary – often the only – service provider. When I am operating in the capacity of business development, I stretch the possibilities to their outer limits. For example, I once booked speaking engagements in San Francisco, Paris, and Las Vegas in the same week. (It's possible.) Flights are available that accommodate being in San Francisco on Monday, Paris on Wednesday, and Las Vegas in Friday while also allowing for time to speak at a conference in each of the cities. Accepting these opportunities is a no-brainer for a sales professional.

When it came time to *deliver* these keynote addresses in three cities on two continents in five days, well that was an entirely different issue. I remember being quite displeased – nay, angry – when I was sitting at the San Francisco International Airport waiting for my flight to Paris. I was already tired and the prospects of two more events and the corresponding travel involved made me even more exhausted. Who would book such a crazy week? Oh, that's right, me. Me, in a business development mode.

Conflict between sales and operations is quite common within organizations. Unfortunately, this lack of seamwork is particularly detrimental to the company's performance potential. There is no more powerful business development resource than a service delivery approach (operations) that collaborates closely with business development (sales) to keep them informed of the client experience and needs. Retaining and expanding the services we provide to existing customers is far and away the most cost-effective component of business development. Capturing more revenues from existing clients results in less pressure to identify, develop, and close new clients. Finding new clients is exponentially more expensive, complicated, and inefficient than growing our existing client base.

Seamwork between sales and operations is not the only inter-departmental relationship that can be unhealthy. Seams exist between all functional units (human resources, accounting, purchasing, sales, service, maintenance, etc.). A leadership ideology that promotes the strengthening of these seams will enhance organizational performance and vertical alignment. This can be achieved through cross training, job sharing, cross departmental meetings, corporate team building, and other devices that generate awareness for the important role each team plays in organizational success. Some companies have gone so far as to fundamentally reshape their organizational structure. Rather than operate with the traditional function-based approach to structure (Figure 4.1), they have created cross-functional teams devoted to specific clients (Figures 4.2 and 4.3). In this model, clients work with their own service team composed of a business development person, a client service liaison, accounts receivable professionals, and a team of service providers. Each of these functions meets to discuss the client needs. In this type of organization, an individual doesn't work in accounting, for example; they work for ABC Client Team, providing accounting services.

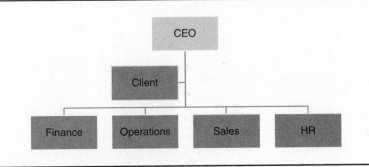

FIGURE 4.1   Traditional structure.

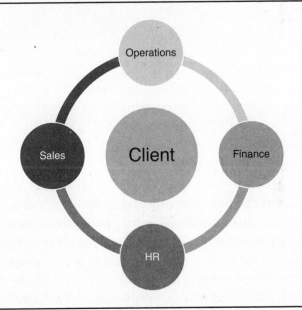

FIGURE 4.2   Seamwork structure: customer centric.

Seamwork doesn't require a radical shift in organizational structure. Seamwork *does* require that the communication between functions is just as strong as the communication within functions. Effective leadership ideology promotes these relationships.

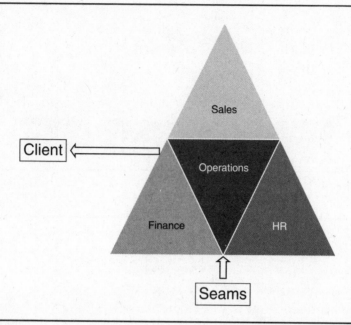

FIGURE 4.3   Seamwork structure: non-customer centric.

LEADERSHIP TOXICITY

As beneficial as the previous eight leadership components are to peak performance culture, there are other qualities that, when manifested by even a single leader, can be devastating. Practically every C-suite leader whom I have met possesses an ample ego. Ego has taken a bit of a beating as a leadership quality in recent years. Like almost everything about human beings, ego has the potential to be beneficial or damaging. Leaders with a strong ego often have clarity and conviction when it comes to their strategies. They are often more resilient – capable to bounce back strong after mistakes. A positively developed ego combined with ample self-examination can result in a confident leader who recognizes her strengths, is comfortable with her shortcomings, and surrounds herself with others to augment her talent. My previous book, *The Power of Understanding Yourself*, examines the importance of metacognition – thinking about how you think – to arrive at your personal mission statement, desired future state, preferred communication style, and the strengths and weaknesses that make you who you are. Leaders with strong egos are particularly in need of defining these qualities.

However, ample ego can be a double-edged sword. Without the balance of self-awareness, leaders can develop toxic characteristics. The most prominent ones that I have witnessed are arrogance, complacency, and trend chasing. The latter two may well be manifestations of the first.

The symptoms of arrogance are easy to spot. Leaders who possess this toxic quality are often dismissive of input from others. They position themselves as the one gifted person driving performance with their infallible vision and strategy. Others are merely pawns for executing their plan. The failure to listen to or solicit feedback from others is indicative of this trait. Often this disinterest in others' perspectives is accompanied by belittling – overt or subtle – of others. One of the most unexpected realizations for me in my career was how many CEOs or senior-level leaders talk critically of their own organization's culture. It doesn't seem to occur to them that they are instrumental in creating the very culture they are criticizing.

Complacency may be an offshoot of arrogance, a reflection of a lack of creativity, or simply denial. It becomes evident in an organization that had a high-performance culture at one time but is clearly losing its competitive edge. The arrogance is indicated by the belief that, regardless of market changes, the way they have always done things will continue to generate success. Or leaders may have no idea how to deal with market changes and their egos prevent them from reaching out for help. Finally, complacency can be the product of an unwillingness to engage in the tough decisions necessary to remain a peak performance culture. After all, changes to horizontal and vertical alignment are usually long, arduous journeys that may not be appealing to a veteran senior leader.

Finally, trend chasing can have the most debilitating effect on the organization. These senior leaders attend a conference or read an article about the most recent panacea for success. They then direct the organization to adopt the approach without proper consideration of whether the strategy is viable and appropriate. They deploy huge resources. Eventually, the leader moves on to a new buzz word, realigning the organization again. The inevitable response among the rank and file becomes "Just wait for this phase to pass." The strategies lose credibility while wasting large amounts of time, effort, and funding. Trend chasers represent the other side of a spectrum that includes complacency. It is as if the trend chasers fear being complacent and err in the opposite extreme.

THE GREAT EIGHT OF BENEVOLENT ACCOUNTABILITY AND PRAGMATIC CREATIVITY

Organizations that achieve their highest performance potential do so not because of words on a poster in the employee cafeteria. They don't profess to care more, display more honesty, or have better teamwork than their competitors. What they do is manifest a leadership ideology that includes:

- Internal locus of control
- An empowerment culture
- Intrinsic needs fulfillment
- Dialectic thinking
- Zero-based thinking
- Coaching and counseling to shift responsibility
- People Preventative Maintenance System
- Seamwork

They also avoid the toxins of leadership: arrogance, complacency, and trend chasing. When your organization has installed all eight of these elements, it will have successfully satisfied the third metric of peak performance culture. You have the foundation of passion, the structure of alignment, and the power of leadership ideology. Now you need some inhabitants to sat-isfy – customers and employees.

Key Considerations

- The ever-popular organizational values are nice words to place on a poster, but they are unlikely to drive peak performance and may even do more harm than good.
- Hire character, train skills, lead style.
- A leadership ideology that reflects benevolent accountability and pragmatic creativity drives peak performance.
- The single most valuable characteristic that an individual can possess is an internal locus of control.
- Organizations that fail to empower their employees, partic-ularly in mid-level management, create unresolved tension between authority and impact.
- Preparing high value employees for leadership roles before they are placed in that responsibility contributes to a peak performance culture.
- Employees have different intrinsic needs based on their inter-active style. It is important for leadership to create an envi-ronment in which all these intrinsic needs are fulfilled.
- Dialogue is essential for conflict resolution. Dialectic thinking is the only approach that encourages dialogue.
- It is important to occasionally step back from the operation and ask yourself, "Knowing what I know now, would I do that again?" Zero-based thinking helps identify performance challenges.
- All performance problems begin as a leadership failure. Only by shifting accountability from the leader to the team member can these performance problems be corrected.
- Peak performing organizations install mechanisms for proac-tively collecting data reflecting the concerns, frustrations, and suggestions of the team members.

- The strength of the organization is determined by the seams between functional units.
- Most leaders have ample egos. It is essential to avoid the potential toxicity of ego – arrogance, complacency, and trend chasing – to create a peak performance culture.

Chapter 5 The Customer Experience

Most organizations seem to view the customer experience as an either/or matter – as in, either they were satisfied, or they weren't. If a customer seems satisfied, then – according to most companies – we have succeeded. If they are not, we failed. That simple, binary perspective oversimplifies the role that customer experience plays in a peak performance culture. The fact of the matter is that there exists a continuum of customer experiences that create four types of customers:

- **The Evangelist:** This is the best version of a customer. They are delighted by your offerings and echo that enthusiasm on social media channels, reviews, and at parties. They are different than your other satisfied clients in that they recruit others to your brand. They are loyal, forgiving of an occasional misstep, and very hard for your competitor to pry away. If you have a loyalty program, they use it without fail. In the wine industry, they join your club. They are a steadfast source of revenues and help you grow your brand by singing your praises to others. They are rare and extremely valuable.

- **The Satisfied Customer:** This is the most common form of customer. They have experienced your products/services and have been satisfied. Maybe not blown away, but not disappointed. They don't refer you to others because, in their mind, you have done nothing particularly impressive to distinguish yourself beyond meeting their expectations. As a result, a competitor who promises more or charges less or is more convenient can quickly take this customer's business from you. Transient in their patronage and not possessing any brand loyalty, these customers become industry currency with competing organizations chasing this revenue around to achieve their short-term fiscal goals rather than identifying how to convert them to Evangelists. Finding a way to move the Satisfied Customer to the Evangelist is a constant discussion in the organizational boardroom.

- **The Heretic Customer:** In my opinion, this is the most underrated and underappreciated customer. Sure, we would like all our customers to be Evangelists, but the reality is that businesses and their ability to execute on their brand promises are imperfect. We are bound to fall short of our customer's expectations on occasion. The Heretic Customer lets us know when we do. That may not be comfortable for us in the moment, but it allows us to practice good service recovery and make improvements to our operation. Often, a positive response to a Heretic Customer can lead them to become an Evangelist. Think about it. In any relationship, you never know how strong it is until something goes wrong. If you prove to your customer that you can effectively fix a problem that they have expressed, it is far more likely that they will remain loyal to you than the average Satisfied Customer.

- **The Unsatisfied Customer:** This is the most dangerous of customers. These are people who have had an unsatisfactory experience with your business but did not bring it to your attention. Rather than manifesting the behaviors of the Heretic Customer, they simply disappear without a word of feedback to you. They do, however, tell a bunch of other current and potential clients about their dissatisfaction. They are damaging to your brand and restrictive to your ability to improve your practices.

The customer experience process is about creating Evangelists out of Satisfied Customers and encouraging Unsatisfied Customers to be Heretic Customers so that you can convert them to Evangelists. In simple terms, the customer experience is about exceeding expectations during critical interactions, having assertive mechanisms for obtaining customer feedback, and executing an exceptional service recovery process when you fall short of the customer's desires.

One quick note: there is a tiny, tiny, tiny number of people who could be assigned to a fifth customer group. This is populated by a demographic that my dad would call "born mean, lived mean, died mean." The percentage of truly irrational, impossible-to-please people is incredibly small. If you have any, be absolutely certain you didn't create them. If you can be certain you didn't, encourage them to try your competitors.

NOT ALL CUSTOMERS ARE ALIKE

Perhaps the biggest challenge for delivering an exceptional customer experience is that the definition of service excellence varies depending on the client. Essentially, all customers want some combination of the following factors from their service provider:

- A relationship with a likeable person who genuinely cares about them
- An efficient solution to their needs that will improve their life
- A knowledgeable professional who can evaluate and recommend the right product and service
- Someone who is willing to explore options and customize their experience

While all customers want all these factors delivered by their service provider, they prioritize them in different orders. Some customers are far more forgiving of a less knowledgeable employee if that person displays a genuine, likeable demeanor. Others, however, have less interest in tolerating a charming service provider if they are inadequately trained. Many customers are far less interested in all the options than they are in a rapid resolution of their specific problem while others do want to engage in an exploration of the possibilities to select the one that most reflects their own lifestyle.

In Chapter 4, "Leadership Ideology," I discussed the importance of intrinsic needs fulfillment and referenced four iconic interactive styles: Romantics, Warriors, Experts, and Masterminds. These styles don't just manifest in employee behaviors. They exist in our customers. Romantic customers prioritize relationships over the other three factors, Warriors want solutions, Experts want knowledge, and Masterminds want options.

High-performing cultures invest in training that enables their service providers to quickly ascertain the way each customer prioritizes the elements of the experience. Further, these cultures evaluate their own products and services to determine what types of customers are attracted to them and why. They evaluate: What is the brand, and whom does it attract? Here's an example.

Roth Living distributes luxury domestic appliances (Sub-Zero, Wolf, etc.) in the Midwest and Mountain states of the United States. They display these beautiful kitchen appliances in showrooms in Denver, St. Louis, Kansas City, Minneapolis, and Salt Lake City. The products are amazing, and the service is impeccable. The incredible part of their business model is that they don't sell any of these appliances. They distribute appliances to retail stores where the consumer can purchase them. So why does Roth Living have these opulent showrooms and create amazing customer experiences, even though they don't sell directly to the end user?

It's about understanding your customer and delivering an experience that is consistent with your brand. In a retail showroom, the brands that Roth Living carries will be displayed next to or near all the other brands. Sometimes they are placed in their own area within the store in an attempt to create a luxury oasis – something Sub-Zero calls a "Living Kitchen" – within a broader showroom, but other times they are side by side with less expensive and less luxurious brands. The customer of that retail store will be working with a sales professional who is expected to know about *all* the brands and models that they carry. Most, if not all, will be far cheaper than the Sub-Zero or Wolf brands. Adding to the challenge, far more customers are searching for appliances below the Sub-Zero and Wolf price points, so retail sales professionals become more knowledgeable on the less-expensive brands and may even develop a cognitive bias toward selling other brands because of this comfort level.

The manufacturer, and Roth Living, can and do invest in training and merchandising support for the retailer, but the ultimate control of the customer experience resides with the store. That means that a Sub-Zero or Wolf customer will likely have exactly the same experience as a client shopping for an entry-level appliance. The luxury market exists not just because of the level of craftmanship of the products, but also the value-added luxury elements that surround the product. That is nearly impossible to deliver at a store that has an inventory across all price points.

Roth Living solves this problem by taking control of the customer experience. They promote their value to the sales professionals as a resource for differentiating the brand without the risk of losing the sale. If you have a customer interested in Sub-Zero and/or Wolf appliances, send them to us, says Roth Living, and we will treat them to an experience matching this client's luxury expectations. Roth Living has essentially inserted itself into the retail transaction to ensure that their customers have a luxury experience that would be impossible for the store's showroom to deliver on. That is a peak-performing customer experience.

It doesn't end there, either. Roth Living knows that the majority of their clients are Warriors and Masterminds. Sure, they have Romantics and Experts, too, but not as many. And we know that Masterminds like options, innovative features, and cool stuff. Roth Living's showrooms are practically a playground for adults – a Mastermind fantasy. For the Warrior, the showroom staff can save them time by quickly using resources to steer them to the exact appliance package to fit their needs – efficient, solution-focused service, all while allowing them to experience the status that plays to their competitive natures.

Therein lies the secret to creating Evangelist customers from satisfied customers – meeting their intrinsic need. A Romantic customer is naturally loyal, provided they have worked with a likeable service provider who appreciates their patronage. Experts don't like mistakes and respond to security, so a knowledgeable service provider who can deliver what they promise will keep their business. Knowing your customer's intrinsic need and fulfilling it will convert a merely satisfied customer to the more valuable Evangelist.

THE HEART AND ART OF SERVICE EXCELLENCE

My career in corporate human resources development was greatly shaped by my experiences at Marshall Field's and Buena Vista Hospitality Group. The common thread between upscale retail and hospitality is the emphasis placed on customer service as a brand differentiator. Both companies took that competitive advantage seriously. My role at both organizations included assuring customer satisfaction by providing both employee training and organizational systems that supported this commitment to the customer experience.

Actually, I think my appreciation for the human element in business can be traced to working for my dad at Mitchell's

Heating and Air Conditioning as a kid. Dale Mitchell sold HVAC and appliances and did some illegal plumbing when necessary. Greenup, Illinois, was a small town. My dad seemed to know every single person in it and could call them by name the moment they walked into his store. He knew their story, created an experience tailored to them, and managed to survive the assault of "big box" stores for several years by embodying his brand promise, "Mitchell's – Where Service Is Our Business." I can recall many occasions on a Sunday or a holiday or in the middle of the night when our home phone would ring and off Dad went to try to fix a furnace, a refrigerator, or an oven for a panicked customer.

Among my responsibilities as a 16-year-old was to send past due statements to the customers who had not paid for their service call or were late on their installment for an appliance they had purchased. Some of these statements represented transactions that were years old, yet my Dad insisted I send them out. Not only that, he would continue to perform service calls or sell these customers more merchandise.

I would ask him, "Why do you continue to provide service to these people if they don't pay their bill?"

"Am I supposed to leave them without heat?" he would say. "They don't have a pot to piss in, so they can't afford to pay me."

"Then why do you bother sending them bills and late notices?" It seemed a waste of time for me to hand scribe the statement, address an envelope, put a stamp on it, and mail it out each month.

"Well, I damn sure want them to remember how much they owe me, even if they don't pay."

That was my dad. He was what I call a Hired Gun (a Warrior/Romantic). He also had a servant's heart.

I can't remember when I first heard the term "servant's heart" but I loved it immediately. Some people do seem to be wired to make others happy. Initially, I thought this quality was linked to Romantics exclusively, but I eventually came to realize that despite their self-sacrificing nature, they are not always natural service providers. All interactive styles have the capacity to flourish as practitioners of service excellence. After all, customers come in all four types, so it is obvious that service providers do, too. Romantic service providers excel at building relationships, Warrior service providers efficiently solve problems, Experts know their stuff, Masterminds get creative. The key is that they have a genuine desire to make people happy. It fulfills them. That is the servant's heart – the heart of service.

A customer experience that creates Evangelists will require an employee base that exhibits a servant's heart. That alone, however, is not enough. There is an art to service as well. That is where employee training is so valuable. The heart of service excellence is best acquired through employee selection processes, but the art can be created through skills training. Teaching people how to acknowledge, greet, treat, and execute the technical aspects of the customer interaction is a necessary part of creating the desired customer experience. An employee with a servant's heart who has not received training in the art of service excellence will quickly become frustrated. It is akin to a carpenter not being given tools or an artist without the resources to create art. Service excellence requires both natural ability and good training.

SERVICE EXCELLENCE AND ORGANIZATIONAL ERGONOMICS

Operational efficiency is one of the success scoreboard metrics. So is customer satisfaction. When these two important components of organizational success misalign, they can create a detrimental customer experience. Sometimes, the process that is most efficient for the organization is *not* conducive to an exceptional customer experience. In the long run, organizations benefit by prioritizing customer experience over operational efficiency if all things are equal. In baseball, the tie goes to the runner. In organizational excellence, the tie goes to the customer.

I personally experienced the mistake of prioritizing efficiency over customer experience with one of my clients. Several years ago, I worked on a project with a national home builder to enhance their customer satisfaction scores. The specific division that was our focus had just finished last in a J. D. Power quality survey of national home builders. I was contracted to collect data from recent home buyers, produce recommendations on training interventions, and deliver the appropriate customer service classes.

We began the project by hosting an open house with recent home buyers to discuss their experience working with the builder. It was a sort of focus group setting without the formality. We served hors d'oeuvres, beer, and wine, and chatted about the highs and lows of the entire process. For anyone who has purchased and built a new home, you know that this whole experience is one of the wildest emotional roller coasters a consumer will experience. The excitement of designing and living in a new home is largely swept away by missed construction deadlines, repeated paperwork requests, and a general sense that nothing is happening until everything happens at once. It is exhausting. As one home builder told me, "Never has the perfect house been built."

Aside from the complaints that were unique to each customer, a common concern emerged from our conversations. Before the customers had signed the contract, their primary service provider was the new home consultant (NHC), the real estate professional who had met them in the model home and steered the sales process from the beginning. The customers found that the NHC was responsive, helpful, and eager to be of service – until the contract was signed and the building process began. Then, responsiveness, helpfulness, and the perception of eagerness waned. It wasn't that the NHC no longer cared about the home buyers; it was that they didn't have the information to answer their questions.

The home's build was the responsibility of the construction manager, a mid-level leader who was responsible for several ongoing homes at various stages of the construction process. When the home buyer would call the NHC, the NHC would have to track down the construction manager to get answers. Often, the construction manager would have to further research the question by contacting supervisors, subcontractors, or inspectors. By the time the NHC could get an answer – *if* they could get an answer – the home buyer was becoming frustrated by the perceived lack of responsiveness. In an interesting example of "behavior breeds behavior," the employee experience was also negatively impacted by this practice. NHCs were complaining about the challenge of obtaining construction updates, and construction managers were irritated by the constant requests for updates from the NHC.

Upon presenting the results of our focus groups to the builder's executive team, we identified a solution. (Side note: the following is a perfect example of the imbalance of authority and impact discussed in the leadership ideology section. Had we spent more time polling the team members and mid-level leaders, we could have made a much better decision.) We decided that the primary contact for the home buyer should shift from the NHC before contract to the construction manager after contract. The thought process here was that the home buyer could receive a quicker, more thorough update from the construction manager and the NHC could focus on driving sales rather than chasing information down for contracted deals. To support the construction managers as they took on direct customer contact, we would put them through a four-part service excellence training program to enhance their customer service skills.

From an operational efficiency standpoint, it made perfect sense. From a customer experience perspective, it seemed to resolve the biggest complaint of home buyers. It even looked good from an employee development angle – enhanced skills for construction managers, more focus on sales for the NHCs, who were compensated based on sold homes. I remember feeling pretty damn good about that meeting.

There was only one problem. Construction managers are not candidates for a servant's heart. Now, don't get me wrong; there are exceptions. However, a construction manager is primarily responsible for getting a home built on time and with quality. This requires overseeing contractors who pour concrete, install plumbing, do electrical work, put up dry wall, paint, landscape, and the like. They are challenged to meet deadlines by holding people accountable, many of whom do not work for them, have other clients, are dealing with their own employee challenges, and so on. In other words, there are a lot of moving parts to building just one home. Construction managers are overseeing *many* home builds. As a result, tact, diplomacy, and patience become less important than demands, threats, and coercion when it comes to getting results. It's not that construction managers are mean; it's just that their interactions with contractors are, um, more spirited than one would desire with a customer.

After the second seminar, it became clear to me that – while eager and willing – this group was just not the right contact point for a home buyer. It was unreasonable to expect the construction manager to seamlessly transition from holding the electrician responsible for a deadline, sending a drywaller home because he smelled like alcohol, negotiating with a home inspector, and then dealing with a nervous home buyer. The behavior breeds behavior tenet was not working in their favor. Add to this situation that the home buyer did not want to change contact people when they'd already built a relationship with the NHC. We had missed the mark by erring on the side of efficiency instead of customer experience.

While not as efficient, the better solution was far more beneficial for the customer experience. Instead of training the construction managers to do something that was not part of their core competency, we designed a system in which the construction managers met with the NHCs each week to update them on the progress of each home. This allowed the NHCs to proactively update the home buyer. If the home buyer had questions that the NHC couldn't answer, they would inform the home buyer that they would get the answer at the next meeting with the construction manager. Home buyers came to expect that the NHC would have updates once a week – a time frame that they felt was reasonable. NHCs could schedule calls with their home buyer around the meetings with construction managers. Construction managers knew they would have one meeting a week with NHCs, rather than receiving several calls about individual homes each day.

This solution was a homerun. Home buyers were more satisfied with the understanding that they would receive weekly updates; NHCs were more comfortable receiving weekly updates and proactively calling home buyers; and construction managers were happier limiting interactions with NHCs to one weekly meeting rather than several daily calls. For what it's worth, the construction managers also enjoyed the training on service excellence but were relieved not to have the responsibility of being the primary contact for home buyers. The construction managers who did have a servant's heart were able to contribute to the home buyers' experience directly if needed. Those who didn't have this orientation could stay out of the picture.

SERVICE RECOVERY

One of the most overlooked aspects of the art of service excellence is handling the Unsatisfied or Heretic Customer. It can be uncomfortable for an organization to admit that they will occasionally fall short of their customers' expectations, but the reality is that it is inevitable. Rather than avoid this unattractive truth, peak performing cultures embrace it. Remember, Heretic Customers – when properly handled – often become Evangelists.

The good news is that service recovery is about as simple as a process can be, especially one that is so critical to the customer experience. Unlike the complexities of interactive style, intrinsic need fulfillment, journey mapping, filtering, and so on, service recovery does have a nice, clean, one-size-fits-all approach. It is so straightforward it even has a fitting acronym: the LAST model.

- **Listen**: Let the customer share their entire complaint. This is important. Do not interrupt, even if you know exactly what to do just five seconds into their rant. It is critical for the customer to express *all* of their frustration. They will often begin to lose their hostility – even become somewhat apologetic for their emotional state – by the end of their diatribe. This step is about two things: understanding the nature of the customer's concern *and* allowing them to vent their emotional response. If you fail to accomplish either, you will not effectively recover.

- **Apologize**: This can be hard, especially if you do not feel the organization is at fault or you do not appreciate the way the customer has engaged. However, the apology is not an admission of culpability so much as the regret that the customer feels the way they do, regardless of blame. When a service provider says, "I am so sorry you are having this experience," it diffuses the remaining anger and establishes an alliance between the employee and the customer. The key to service recovery is to realign with the customer rather than maintain what has evolved into an adversarial relationship. Once the customer views us as an ally, we will no longer be the object of their scorn.

- **Solve**: This is critical. A customer is only a customer if we are providing them with a product or service of value. For this reason, I encourage my clients to adopt a policy of "Never say no." If we cannot solve their problem, we have no value. A hard *no* to a client will either end the relationship or force them to explore other avenues to get value, like asking to speak to the manager. On those rare occasions that we have decided to part ways with a customer – those people who were born mean, lived mean, died mean – only a person with ultimate authority should be involved. Service providers should always be providing service.

Now, "Never say no" is not the same thing as "Always say yes." It is important that service providers are allowed (and trained on) a broad latitude of options for resolving a customer's dissatisfaction. I find it best if customers are given choices as to how they would like their concern resolved. This gives the power back to the consumer and allows for a satisfactory reconciliation within the parameters of the organization's practices. Bottom line on customer complaints: if the customer wants something that we can provide, give it to them. If we can't provide what they ask for, offer them three options that you can.

- **Thank:** If you thought apologizing to a dissatisfied client was tough, imagine how hard thanking them will be. This is the step that is most often omitted and yet it is essential to creating Evangelists. Remember, most Unsatisfied Customers leave us without telling us. Yet many *do* tell other people through social media posts, word of mouth, and the myriad other ways we can express ourselves today. When a customer shares their criticism of us *to us*, that is incredibly useful. Not only does it allow us to win them back, but it provides important feedback about our operation – hence, why Heretics are so valuable.

Training your entire organization on the LAST model of service recovery and all the other procedural elements of customer service will create a peak performance culture based on both the heart and the art of service excellence.

CUSTOMER JOURNEY MAPPING AND THE POWER OF EXPECTATIONS

Beyond the interactive style and intrinsic needs considerations of the client is the notion of understanding customer expectations. We often evaluate whether we've met, exceeded, or fell short of customer expectations using broad measures. Customer satisfaction scores, net promoter scores, and online reviews are typical metrics that organizations use to gauge the effectiveness of the customer experience. However, customers do not assess their interaction with the organization as one big experience. Rather, a customer's opinion of your organization is formed over time based on a series of critical interactions with the operation and employees. Understanding a couple of key terms and their importance to the customer experience is necessary.

Anticipated Experience

Each customer forms an imaginary (anticipated) version of how their interaction with your organization will go before that experience occurs. This version is influenced by several factors. One is the organization's marketing messages (websites, commercials, advertisements). It is common for a company to represent itself through marketing at the height of its capabilities. Some may represent themselves in a manner that exceeds their capacity to deliver (you can refer to my story in the chapter on vertical alignment for an example of the dangers of overpromising the brand). This can create a difficult and potentially insurmountable expectation in the consumer's mind. Marketing that overpromises on the actual customer experience can be detrimental to the company's long-term success.

A second factor for forming the customer's anticipated experience with your organization comprises the experiences this customer has had with competitors or with situations or businesses like yours. For example, if a customer is visiting a winery, they will likely anticipate an experience that is formed by the previous wine tasting rooms they have visited. They may also imagine elements of related food and beverage experiences like breweries, restaurants, and even grocery stores.

Another factor is the reputation created by online reviews, others' opinions, and the input of specifiers and influencers of the consumer. Referrals are a powerful component of the anticipated experience. If others whom customers trust have told them good things about your company, they elevate their expectations. Of course, the opposite is true as well. In the latter situation, the customer may never choose to be a patron of your business – reaffirming the damage of the Unsatisfied Customer.

Achieving and maintaining an exceptional customer experience can be particularly challenging for this very reason. As your reputation elevates, so do expectations and customers' anticipated experience. While we should always strive to increase our customers' expectations, there is no denying that as the customer's anticipated experience becomes more elaborate and demanding, it places pressure on our ability to meet and/or exceed it. Fortunately, there are some "hacks" that can make accomplishing that a little easier.

Critical Interactions

Each customer experience is a composite of flashpoints – critical interactions – that collectively form the customer's opinion of the transaction. For example, a stay at a hotel begins when the guest sees the hotel from the road – the curbside appeal. The customer then may choose to park their car and begin the process of transitioning from car to hotel via the parking lot and porte cochere. Next, they enter the lobby, then check in at the front desk, followed by traveling from the lobby to their guest room, and finally they enter their room. Each of these flashpoints—curb appeal, parking transition, lobby, front desk process, trip to guest room, and guest room itself – represents a critical interaction with the hotel operation. Each is an opportunity to meet expectations, exceed them, or fall below the customer's anticipated experience.

Journey Mapping

A useful, perhaps even necessary, exercise is the process of identifying these critical interactions common to most customer experiences, and then defining the anticipated experience an average customer would imagine. Of course, "average customer" is a tough metric. Still, if you can evaluate your marketing brand, competitive experiences, potential analogous experiences, and your existing reputation, you can create a meaningful anticipated experience for each critical interaction.

High-performing organizations often use two mechanisms to assist in the process of mapping the customer journey and defining the anticipated experience: client advisory boards and client awareness councils. I will examine these two committees in more detail later, but either or both can be instrumental in creating an accurate customer journey map.

Journey mapping not only defines the anticipated experience for each critical interaction; it also identifies the chronology of these interactions and potential branches that a customer experience may involve. Most customer experiences are not simple, linear maps, but rather a series of options that can move their interactions in different directions.

For example, a hotel guest may be a leisure traveler who spends significant time using the recreational amenities like pools, tours, and restaurants, or a business traveler who spends much of their time in meeting rooms, business centers, and banquet meals. The best customer journey mapping can plot most if not all the many directions the critical interactions can take. It can be an arduous task to examine the multitude of potential interactions a single client can have with your organization. This is why having both internal (employee) and external (customer) committees involved in the mapping is so important.

Once completed, a customer journey map should be augmented to include two more components critical to enhancing the customer experience. Each critical interaction should be evaluated using a process like a SWOT analysis. By doing a quick review of the organizational strengths, weaknesses, opportunities, and threats at every component of the customer experience, you can anticipate the potential ways that the customer may receive service that exceeds or fails to meet their expectations. By identifying the ways that the critical interaction may fail to meet the customer expectations, you can proactively address any weaknesses and threats. By seeing how the critical interaction may *exceed* the customer expectations, you can now do a cost benefit analysis of potential changes to your service delivery. The goal is not to make *every* critical interaction exceed a customer's expectation – this can become very expensive to the organization. The goal is to strategically target critical interactions that occur early in the customer experience and can effectively create a positive filter within the customer for future interactions. The concept of filtering is important to creating Evangelists and Satisfied Customers.

Filtering

Once a customer begins experiencing our services, they start comparing their actual experience to the anticipated experience. As is the case when we meet a person for the first time, early impressions are very influential in forming our opinions. As the customer begins the journey through our operation, they are continually comparing their actual experience to the previously formed anticipated experience. If the actual experience matches what the customer anticipated, this is a neutral interaction. We have neither improved nor diminished their opinion of us. Neutral critical interactions are quite useful in that they do no harm; however, they have not enhanced the likelihood that this customer will view us positively. Using the hotel stay example from above, if the customer's first glimpse of the property – the curb appeal – matches their anticipated experience, the guest has neither a positive nor negative reaction.

If the actual experience during a critical interaction exceeds the customer's anticipated experience, then we have achieved a positive interaction. Not only is this good news for that interaction, but if you can string together a few early positive critical interactions, you'll influence subsequent interactions. This is called filtering. Once a customer installs a positive filter for their experience, the result of having several early positive interactions, they become more likely to view us in a positive light on subsequent interactions. This makes them more forgiving of future critical interactions as they subconsciously seek positive information to reinforce their filter. They literally look for the good in future interactions.

Individuals who experience critical interactions that fall below their anticipated experience have a negative interaction. Stringing a few of these together runs the risk of creating a negative filter in the client. Once a negative filter is installed, customers are more likely to seek out more negative information to reinforce that filter. While it is possible to change a customer's filter, it becomes much harder to create a positive customer experience if they possess a negative filter. For this reason, it is important to spend significant time evaluating the initial critical interactions involving the customer. If the organization can successfully install a positive filter in the customer early in the relationship, they will have built both goodwill and bias in their favor to protect them against any future interactions that are less favorable.

Client Advisory Boards

Client Advisory Boards (CABs) are populated by passionate customers who want to contribute to the success of the organization. The composition of the CAB is of critical importance. The temptation, rightfully so, is to populate this committee with Evangelists of the organization. That's typical. I would suggest that one of the values of creating a Client Advisory Board is to *create* Evangelists, so selecting only those customers who already reflect this level of commitment to the organization doesn't broaden your population of these influential clients. While a few Evangelists on the Client Advisory Board are very useful, consider populating the committee mostly with Satisfied Customers and carefully chosen Heretics, too. Remember, Heretics are passionate and will provide a valuable counterpoint to the Evangelists. When selecting Heretics to be part of the Client Advisory Board, be sure to vet them thoroughly. You want open-minded, reasonable and genuine clients who appreciate your desire to improve your operation. What you don't want is someone with an axe to grind who will use the CAB meetings as an opportunity to rail against the organization and potentially poison other customers.

Relative to composition, it is valuable to populate the CAB with diverse styles of consumers: Romantics, Warriors, Experts, and Masterminds. This ensures that all types of customer perspectives are represented. It also means that your Client Advisory Board will be spirited in debate, and that consensus may be difficult to achieve. Remember, a CAB is an *advisory* board, not a mandate board. The key is to listen intently to their feedback and then make your own decisions about how to use their information.

The primary value of a CAB is to clearly define the anticipated experience for each critical interaction. Once this has been accomplished, the CAB can become a sort of test group for discussing ideas for enhancing select critical interactions to exceed customer's expectations.

Client Awareness Councils

A Client Awareness Council (CAC) is an employee committee that is composed of individuals from a cross section of corporate functions. Each major division of the organization should be represented. Their purpose duplicates some of the CAB's role in that they, too, will perform customer journey mapping, discuss anticipated experience, and recommend strategic improvements to generate actual experiences that exceed the customer expectation and create a positive filtering effect. This group can also elevate awareness for the customer perspective within their work units, develop organization wide promotional efforts for the customer experience, and serve as a conduit for issues related to the employee experience discussed in the following chapter.

Here is a sample list of responsibilities for a CAC (in this case a PAC, a Patient Awareness Council) for one of my pharmaceutical clients, Piramal Pharma Solutions:

- Increase awareness of how our work impacts a patient.
- Promote best practices for a patient centric operation.
- Identify opportunities to improve operational practices to enhance patient centricity.
- Document operational enhancements that improve patient centricity.
- Report operational enhancements to executive level.
- Schedule monthly meetings with site director to update on efforts and make recommendations.

As is the case with Client Advisory Boards, selecting the right people to serve on the CAC is essential. These individuals should represent some of the highest performers in the organization who are respected by all employees regardless of position and influence. While they will be obvious advocates of the customer, they must have a genuine desire to improve the organization. This means they must be confident enough to question policies and procedures within their own department and curious enough to explore how areas outside their work function impact the customer experience. One of the most challenging aspects of the customer experience is navigating the seamwork within an organization.

Seamwork was discussed at length in Chapter 4, "Leadership Ideology." The concept can have a significant impact on the customer experience. One of the consistent complaints I hear from sales professionals is the frustration of working hard to win a client's business, only to have an order fulfilled inaccurately, delivered later than promised, or some other misalignment of the service promise versus the service experience. Of course, this can be an example of sales creating an expectation that is impossible for the organization to deliver on. Regardless of who is to blame, the customer experience almost always involves crossing many functional work groups within the organization. If any one of those work groups fails to deliver, the entire customer experience is affected. The Client Awareness Council must be prepared to cross through the functional boundaries of the organization to strengthen the seamwork. Here is a list of considerations for selecting members of the PAC referenced above:

The council should comprise 8–12 members who reflect diversity of all types, including interactive style and job responsibilities. When selecting candidates, please consider the following qualities:

- High-performing employee
- Respected and influential among peers
- A natural leader but not necessarily in leadership role in organization
- Confident and comfortable with engaging in critical thinking related to company processes
- Exceptional communication skills
- Displays a patient centric mentality already
- Displays core values of knowledge, action, care, and impact
- Reliable
- Enthusiastic about the opportunity to serve on the council

The Lifespan of Boards and Councils

Both Client Advisory Boards and Client Awareness Councils entail a diverse group of people with a shared interest in organizational success but disparate perspectives. Trying to unify individuals with differing points of view but a shared responsibility involves some easy-to-anticipate challenges. Psychological researcher Bruce Tuckman famously identified the stages of development as "forming, storming, norming, and performing." Here's what I have observed as it relates to group dynamics surrounding diverse individuals with a common purpose.

Propulsion

During this stage, the group is assembled and given their purpose. Typically (and importantly) the group has been selected using criteria that ensure each individual reflects the correct attributes desired for this team (see the example list above). Because the group members are highly engaged peak performers, there is no shortage of energy and ideas at the council or board's inception. Enthusiasm is high, contributions are plentiful, and the "buzz" is palpable.

Confusion

During about the third or fourth meeting, some degree of chaos begins to emerge. This can be the result of too many ideas being introduced, a lack of clarity about roles and priorities among the group, the realization that results will be less immediate than originally expected, and so on. There's a very real risk that the group veers off their intended purpose. Often it is during this stage of development that clarifications are needed and the group must be rebooted.

Frustration

Confusion left uncorrected will lead to bickering, power struggles, failed initiatives, and cliques of dissension. This is the most dangerous stage for the group as it has reached a crossroads. Strong leadership will be necessary to navigate the direction moving forward.

Revision or Division

The correct path moving forward is to revisit the board or council's original charter and evaluate the efforts so far. Often revision is needed between six months and one year after propulsion. Failure to take time to revise the council's efforts can create further division caused by the frustration of the previous stage. This division will eventually be terminal to the group.

Reignition or Dissolution

Upon revising efforts and regaining clarity on the board or council's purpose, the group can now regain their enthusiasm for its mission. Often new members are brought in to replace members who have lost energy or were miscast. Reignition does not restart the stages; it begins a second, more effective version of the group that has been enhanced by experience, knowledge, and better composition. Dissolution is the result of a failure to revise, renovate, and reignite the group. The disfunction of the council or board is too prevalent to overhaul without a complete makeover. When a group reaches this stage, it is best to start over.

What is interesting to me is that all groups experience confusion and frustration. These are not indicators of a dysfunctional council or board. The critical factor is how leadership responds to these stages. Using confusion and frustration as a signal to reexamine the charter, evaluate successes and failures, and revise approaches and composition will lead to an even more effective group. Failure to do so will effectively terminate it.

The Need for a CAB and CAC

A key to the effectiveness of both Client Advisory Boards and Client Awareness Councils is to develop a reporting structure that reaches the highest levels of the organization. Minimally, the organization should assign the responsibility of the customer experience to a C-suite-level executive. Optimally, this position should be exclusively responsible for customer centricity. A happy medium is expanding the highest sales executive's role to include the customer experience. In the Piramal Pharma Solutions example, Stu Needleman serves as the Chief Commercial Officer (sales) and Chief Patient Centricity Officer (customer experience). Having a voice at the executive board level helps ensure that the work of CABs and CACs is more than just lip service and provides meaningful organizational direction.

You will find examples of the PAC charter and welcome letter for your reference at the end of this chapter. These documents were created with the input of Paul Delfino. Delfino Marketing Communications, the Leadership Difference, Inc., and Piramal Pharma Solutions working together on this initiative.

The value of having both a CAB and CAC is that the two entities provide distinctly different perspectives operationally. The CAB views the operation from the outside in, while the CAC sees it from inside out. Creating the best possible customer experience in a manner that is cost effective, consistent, and sustainable will require that these two perspectives are balanced. Not lost in all this is that the customer experience is most often about people serving people. Remember, as discussed in Chapter 2, "Horizontal Alignment," behavior breeds behavior – the origin of that phrase will be explained in our next chapter. Ultimately, the customer experience will be indelibly influenced by the employee who is delivering the service. That employee's behavior will be influenced by the way the organization treats them. So, the employee experience impacts the customer experience. Unfortunately, most organizations don't treat the two anywhere near the same.

Sample of Piramal Pharma Solutions Charter
Patient Awareness Council Charter, December 9, 2019, v1.0

The Mission of the Patient Awareness Council

At Piramal Pharma Solutions, everything we do, we do for the patient. Patients are the common purpose that we at Piramal Pharma Solutions share with our customers. To be the best possible partner for our customers, it is vital that we embrace patient centricity as our mindset and culture. It's much more than a marketing slogan – it's why we do what we do.

Patient centricity aligns with Piramal's core values:

- Knowledge: a deeper understanding of patients' needs and concerns
- Action: for the good of others
- Care: concern for the personal side of drug development
- Impact: operational improvements, improved quality

In order to ensure that the strategy of patient centricity is embraced across the organization, we are establishing volunteer Patient Awareness Councils at each Piramal Pharma Solutions site around the world. At their core, the councils serve an important mission: to drive advocacy and awareness of patient centricity and to suggest operational changes that can bring this initiative to life.

Council Structure

Each Piramal Pharma Solutions site will have its own council comprised of 8–12 site employees who represent a wide breadth of interactive styles and job responsibilities. Candidates who choose to volunteer to serve on their site's council should demonstrate the following qualities:

- Respected and influential among peers
- A natural leader, but not necessarily in a leadership role in the organization
- Confident and comfortable with engaging in critical thinking related to company processes
- Strong communication skills
- Currently display a patient-centric mentality
- Understand and exhibit Piramal Pharma Solutions core values of knowledge, action, care, and impact
- Demonstrate reliability
- Enthusiastic about the opportunity to serve on the council

Council Responsibilities

Council members will be expected to be the voice of patient centricity at their site, with specific functional responsibilities that include:

- Manifest the momentum for change.
- Increase awareness among staff of how our work impacts a patient, including information about the products made and their importance to patients.
- Promote best practices for a patient-centric operation.

- Address the specific challenges that exist at each site relative to patient centricity.
- Identify opportunities to improve operational practices to enhance patient centricity.
- Document operational enhancements that improve patient centricity.
- Report operational enhancements to the executive level.
- Provide regular updates on activity to the site head, including recommended actions.
- Report on metrics as defined by the Chief Patient Centricity Officer (these may include customer satisfaction, customer retention, Net Promoter Score, operational improvements, fiscal performance, etc.).

Selection Process and Leadership

Participation as a council member is voluntary. Each site's council should have no fewer than 8 members and no more than 12, established via this process:

- Each site head will nominate a chairperson for their site's council.
- The chairperson will solicit volunteers from across the site.
- The chairperson, site head, and a representative of HR will evaluate candidates against the criteria shown above and select from the volunteers.
- If there are not enough volunteers, or if some key functional areas are not represented, the chairperson, site head, and HR rep may target specific individuals and ask for their participation.
- A vice chairperson, who will serve as chair in the absence of the chairperson, will be elected by vote at the council kickoff meeting for each site.

Council Meeting Protocols

Council members will be daily advocates of the patient while demonstrating PPS's core values.

- Once established, each council will be provided with guidelines and expectations for their kickoff meeting by the Chief Patient Centricity Officer.
- To ensure that the councils work as an autonomous group, neither the site head nor the Chief Patient Centricity Officer will participate in council meetings.
- The chairperson will be responsible for running each meeting. If unable to participate, the vice chair will assume that responsibility.
- The council chairperson will be responsible for organizing regular meetings of his or her council – no less than once per month – to accomplish the following:
    - Create awareness of the patient perspective for each project.
    - Ensure operational systems and processes recognize the impact they have on the well-being of the patient.
    - Continually promote intended results for improving and saving lives.
    - Stress the importance of meeting customer expectations for project delivery.
    - Display the commitment to making a difference in the people waiting for our work.
- Council feedback, including recommendations on actions, must be presented to the site head and Chief Patient Centricity Officer following each meeting via an in-person meeting, email summary, or teleconference briefing.
- Periodically, all the councils will meet either face to face or by phone to share best practices, discuss their activities, and

deliberate on operational improvements. There will also be opportunities to present specific developments and projects to the PPS executive committee.

Training

After the councils have been populated, members will receive training on the following skills to enhance their ability to succeed:

- Overview of organizational development principles
- The purpose of the patient centricity strategy
- The role of the Patient Awareness Council in the patient centricity strategy
- Discussion of the metrics of success for patient centricity strategy
- Election of a site council chairperson, vice chairperson, and outline of reporting structure to site director and Chief Patient Centricity Officer.

Council Expectations

Council members are expected to abide by these terms:

- Membership on the council is for a minimum term of one year and a maximum term of three years.
- Additional term(s) may be added at the discretion of the site head, Chief Patient Centricity Officer, and HR representative.
- Council members should attend and participate in all council meetings. If unable to attend a meeting due to schedule conflicts, business travel, holiday, or other reason, the council member should notify the chairperson in advance of the meeting.
- If/when the chairperson is unable to attend a meeting, the vice chairperson will assume responsibility for management of that meeting.

- Any council member who misses an excessive number of meetings or otherwise does not contribute to the objectives of the council may be asked to resign from the council at the discretion of the chairperson, site head, and/or HR representative.

Questions? Suggestions? Comments?

Contact Stu Needleman, Chief Patient Centricity Officer, at stuart.needleman@piramal.com

Example of Patient Awareness Council Welcome Letter

Dear [name]

Welcome to the Piramal Pharma Solutions [site name] Patient Awareness Council!

The success of the Patient Awareness Council is extremely important to the company, so your participation on the council should be viewed as both an honor and a privilege. It comes with a mission: to drive advocacy and awareness of patient centricity at your site and all PPS sites around the world, and to suggest operational changes that can bring patient centricity to life.

As a Patient Awareness Council member, you will be expected to be the voice of patient centricity at your site. This means increasing awareness of how our work impacts patients; identifying and promoting best practices; addressing the challenges that exist at each site head-on; and more. Most importantly, it means being an agent for change wherever and whenever the existing culture and site operations are not patient centric.

More information about the specifics of the council – including roles and responsibilities, council structure, meeting protocols, and more – can be found in the Patient Awareness Council Charter document, which you should have already received. Please read it carefully and feel free to address any questions directly with me.

The next step for council members is onboarding and training. In my role as Chief Patient Centricity Officer for the company, I will be working with Dave Mitchell to facilitate training that will provide the council with the information and tools required to make it an effective resource. The training session for your site is scheduled for [insert actual day/time/venue here]. A representative of the site leadership team will be sending out a calendar invitation for the training; please let them know ASAP if you will be unable to attend.

Following the training, the council meetings will begin in earnest. During the initial meeting, council members will be tasked with electing a vice chairman, who will serve as chair in the absence of the chairperson. Each council meeting should also have a member designated to capture notes and action items.

Once again, congratulations on your participation and welcome. I sincerely appreciate your decision to join me on the journey to bring patient centricity to Piramal Pharma Solutions.

Stu Needleman
CPCO and CCO

Key Considerations

- Allot substantial time and resources to create a detailed customer journey map complete with each branch the customer can potentially travel.
- For each critical interaction in the customer journey, identify the neutral experience.
- Identify opportunities to cost effectively enhance critical interactions, paying particular attention to those that occur early in the experience.

- How we recover from a poor customer experience is just as important to our success as our ability to deliver service excellence the first time. All service providers should be trained on service recovery.
- What customers of our organization should populate our Client Advisory Board?
- What criteria should we use to select members for our Client Advocacy Council?
- How will the work of the CAB and CAC inform decisions at the executive level?
- Consider who should provide "executive sponsorship," giving particular consideration to someone who is willing to passionately promote the customer's perspective at the highest levels of the organization.

Chapter 6 The Employee Experience

My career in human resources development took a huge step forward in the spring of 1986 when I was officially hired by Marshall Field and Company. I had worked with them indirectly since 1984 as I was employed by one of their partners, Platt Music Corporation. Platt managed the electronics department for Marshall Field's, and I had worked my way from a customer service representative to their lone training and development professional over a two-year span. When Marshall Field's recruited me to join what was considered at the time to be one of the premier retail employee training and development operations, I was giddy.

Being a training professional navigating the onboarding and training process as a new hire is a distinctly meta experience. You are simultaneously trying to assimilate all the information while evaluating it to make recommendations for enhancement. Few professional experiences have stuck with me as clearly as my first day of new hire orientation at the Old Orchard store in

Skokie, Illinois. The trainer whom I was replacing due to promotion introduced a customer service video produced by John Cleese's company. Yes, for you Monty Python and *A Fish Called Wanda* fans, *that* John Cleese. An updated version of the video, "If Looks Could Kill," still exists to this day. I remember watching it and thinking, "This is exactly how training should be done, entertaining and educational." Perhaps it was that video that would be the subconscious muse for my company's tagline, "Laugh and Learn!" But that's another story.

More important as it relates to the employee experience, that video introduced me to the three tenets of human behavior – or as John Cleese would spell it, "behaviour." Those tenets are:

- Behavior breeds behavior.
- You choose your behavior.
- Positive behavior is more powerful than negative behavior.

Okay, so the last one is my interpretation of the actual video content based on the thirty-plus years of experiences since that orientation class. The point is, the way we treat others has a powerful influence on the way they treat us *and* treat the next person with whom they interact. While the impact of behavior may not always be immediate, people who are treated poorly will eventually treat others poorly. The reason that is so important in peak performance organizations is one of the most overlooked metrics.

Virtually every company I work with places a high emphasis on – or at least pays tremendous lip service to – customer satisfaction. Customer centricity has evolved from an ideology to a necessity. Somehow, however, organizations have failed to understand that they cannot achieve high levels of customer satisfaction, engagement, and enthusiasm if their own employees don't also feel satisfied, engaged, and enthusiastic. Behavior breeds behavior. An apathetic workforce will never produce delighted customers. Gone are the days when a mere paycheck sufficed for ensuring employee satisfaction.

The challenge with creating an exceptional employee experience is that it is necessarily different than the customer experience. As my father was fond of saying when I complained about work, "That's why you get paid. If you liked it, you would have to pay them." That may have been true a few generations ago, but for the last couple of iterations of the work force, people expect an employment experience that transcends just the compensation.

A few years after my experiences at Marshall Field's, I found myself working at a luxury resort and spa in Orlando. In 1990, the Buena Vista Palace was one of the most impressive properties in Central Florida. The grounds were lavishly landscaped, the lobby was luxurious, and everything about the property was designed to impress. The effort to create a positive experience for the guest was evident. However, the resort's employees did not come in the front door, past the landscaping and into the lavish lobby. No, they entered the hotel through the employee entrance, next to the dock and just past the trash dumpsters. Their exposure to the property was mostly via the back hallways, which were clean but hardly luxurious. Rather than witnessing the meticulous service and amenities afforded the guests, employees passed housekeeping, laundry, stewarding, engineering, and all the pragmatic elements that combined to create the magic occurring in the "front of the house."

It was easy to assume that the employees must be so proud to represent such a wonderful resort. "You are so lucky to work at such a beautiful place!" people would often say. Sure, there were worse places to work, but the reality is that the components for an exceptional employee experience are far different than those for the customer. That is why it is critical to understand the items that combine to create high levels of employee engagement and recognize that any company's "back of the house" is just as important as but fundamentally different than the customer-facing version. Just as we complete a journey map for customers, so should we for employees. Since behavior breeds behavior, the way we treat our employees will determine how they treat our customers. The process is different, however. For customers, the journey is transactional and mostly linear. For employees, it is more conceptual and systemic.

The topics explored in our previous chapters all have a bearing on the employee experience. Genuine passion emanating from the highest levels of the organization will inspire and inform the employee perspective. A well-articulated core ideology that is horizontally aligned and well communicated to the rank and file instills pride and clarity among the team. Vertical alignment adds consistency and reasonableness to the policies, procedures, and practices. An exceptional leadership ideology is critical to coaxing high performance from co-workers. Happy customers also create happy employees.

However, there are some additional components unique to the employee that merit our examination. In assessing the effectiveness of an organization in its efforts to create an exceptional employee experience, I "journey map" five key areas.

RECRUITING AND SELECTION

There are three types of organizations as it relates to recruiting and selection. The first type is the company that has absolutely no process for identifying and selecting new talent until they have an opening. These organizations scramble when the sudden need for a new team member emerges. They start from scratch each time, inventing new ways to try to unearth future contributors and overthink the selection process with unnecessary interview components and applicant criteria. This approach is bad in any economic condition, but it is especially devastating when the market environment conspires to limit qualified applicants. The end result of this willful ignorance of the importance of a strong and systematized recruiting and selection process is that job openings take longer to fill, leaders are sucked into the functional responsibilities that they are supposed to be leading, staff is strained, performance suffers, and, finally, the pressure to fill the positions becomes so great that the organization compromises on their standards and hires underqualified applicants. An even worse result can happen when the leader manages to somewhat effectively cover for the loss of a team member to such an extent that the organization decides not to replace them. This self-limiting decision erodes performance at two levels of the organization: the line level and mid-level leadership. Both options – filling an opening with a substandard new hire or choosing to force leadership to cover dual responsibilities – are toxic to peak performance.

I wish I could say that this was an uncommon approach to recruiting and selection. My experience indicates that it is not. In fact, the word "recruiting" isn't applicable to most organizations to which I have been exposed. Recruiting indicates an ongoing effort to promote the organization as a viable, even preferable, place of employment. Few organizations engage in a concerted effort to position themselves as an "employer of choice" within their market. Even those that do often wait until they have a need for a new hire to engage in these activities. For a large percentage of organizations, the recruiting and selection strategy is some variation of "We'll deal with that when the time comes." Sadly, that time comes far too often.

Think of recruiting this way: the customer experience and the employee experience are indelibly connected. For one to be satisfied, so must the other. The strategy for satisfying each may be subtly different, but it will be analogous. As it relates to customers, you are always promoting yourself to ensure that you attract and retain them. The same is true about employees. A peak-performing organization is always promoting the employment experience to create a perpetual supply of interested talent for future openings. More on this later.

The second approach to recruiting and selection reflects a thoughtful process of searching the available employee market and applying a consistent process for evaluating interested and qualified candidates. Good organizational development strategies are applied, including the following:

- Utilizing a fully integrated awareness campaign (social media, job postings, academic institution partners to promote job openings, other advertising media, etc.)

- Updating the job description for accuracy
- Constructing interview questions that will be used for each applicant
- Identifying the organization's team member(s) to be involved in the interview process
- Conducting interview skills training for each team member involved in the process
- Prioritizing identification and selection of new team members for all involved in the process
- Executing the plan efficiently to compress the length of time the job opening exists

Organizations performing these seven functions have achieved the foundation for an effective recruiting and selection program. However, peak performance organizations don't just do the basics. There are two important components of recruiting and selection that separate a peak performance approach from one that is merely effective.

Ongoing Recruitment

First, peak performance organizations are continuously recruiting regardless of current staffing needs. In the first two examples, there is a stark difference in their response to having an opening. The first company scrambles while the second company employs an organized, thoughtful strategy. But both are reacting to a need. Peak performance organizations are proactive, not reactive. They don't wait until they have a need. Peak performance organizations maintain an awareness of the talent both within their industry and in related fields. They are members of professional organizations; partners with local universities, community colleges, and even high schools; and active networkers in the community (both real and virtual via social media platforms).

Further, peak performance organizations encourage their leaders to develop their own replacements inside the organization. When I left the corporate world, I gave a one-year notice. Part of that was to better prepare to start my company, but an even bigger reason was to identify and prepare my replacement. It turns out that I had done a poor job of grooming my own replacement. And by failing to effectively develop my own successor, I had also hamstrung my own career. Peak performance organizations encourage a culture in which leaders develop their own replacements, so that leaders are free to prepare themselves for the next challenge.

How will you know when you have achieved this element of peak performance culture in the area of recruiting and selection? Ask each leader for the names of three candidates who should at least be considered for their job if they were to leave or be promoted. Sounds a little uncomfortable, huh? If it does, that says something about your culture already, and you may want to reread Chapter 4, "Leadership Ideology." In the best organizations, leaders should be aware of a few candidates, both inside and outside the company, whom they would approach to fill an opening before they have a need, even if that opening is their own job.

Imagining the Ideal Candidate

Second, and almost embarrassing in its obviousness, is that peak-performing organizations have a clear idea of what they are looking for in a new hire before they begin the process of identifying and selecting the person. I say that this is almost embarrassing because you would think that all organizations do this. They don't. Despite having a consistent process for identifying and selecting new team members, most organizations still operate with the "I will know them when I meet them" mentality of employee selection. They may clearly identify the job, the interview questions, the process of screening – all the technical parts of the approach – but if you ask the hiring authority to describe the perfect candidate, they struggle.

Subtle distinctions are the difference between adequate performance and peak performance. Focusing on the selection process and achieving those seven items bulleted above will result in adequate performance. Adding an ongoing recruiting strategy and perfect candidate profile will take you to the next level. The perfect candidate profile involves asking the hiring authority to describe that perfect candidate in terms of skills, style, experience, education, and so on. This candidate may not exist, but your best hope for finding this person will be to clearly define them. We do this for many other big decisions in our life. If you have ever bought a house, you probably imagined the perfect one. You may have even written down these details, things like number of bedrooms, number of bathrooms, size of yard, location, quality of school system, commute distance, and so on. The actual house may not have been exactly as you imagined, but you found something much closer to perfect by defining what perfection was to you. Peak performance organizations spend time defining the perfect candidate to add to their team before they begin the search.

By creating a profile of the perfect candidate, you also achieve greater alignment and consensus among all the individuals involved in the hiring process and minimize the risk of hiring based on rapport rather than abilities. The greatest threat to hiring the right person is falling victim to rapport bias. It is easy to mistake a quick and easy interpersonal connection for actual evidence of qualifications. By defining the qualities desired in the successful candidate, you can diminish the impact of rapport. You also make sure that all people involved in the process are evaluating the same qualities rather than just the ones that *they* may feel are important.

If we update our bullet points for an adequate recruiting and selection process to include the two components associated with peak performance cultures, our final checklist for the beginning of the employee experience would look like this:

Recruiting and Selection Checklist

- All leaders maintain a database of potential new hire candidates for their own and team member positions in the event of job openings.
- Utilize a fully integrated awareness campaign (social media, job postings, academic institution partners to promote job openings, other advertising mediums, etc.).
- Create perfect candidate profile for ideal new hire.
- Update the job description for accuracy.
- Construct interview questions that we will use for each applicant.
- Identify the organization's team member(s) to be involved in the interview process.
- Conduct interview skills training for each team member involved in the process.
- Prioritize identification and selection of new team member for all involved in the process.
- Execute the plan efficiently to compress the length of time the job opening exists.

Assessing an Applicant's Locus of Control

One last but very important thought on the employee recruiting and selection process. As I mentioned in Chapter 4, "Leadership Ideology" – and in each of my previous three books – one of the most important qualities in any peak performance culture is possessing an internal locus of control. The goal of the organization is that all employees, not just leadership, manifest this characteristic. It is a quality that is very hard to instill in someone who does not currently possess it. While it may be possible to coach someone *toward* an internal locus of control, it is much easier to simply hire people who already possess it.

I have found that a simple question during the interview process can elicit a surprisingly accurate gauge of an applicant's locus of control. That question is "Tell me about a time you disappointed your boss." Known as a negative balance inquiry, this style of question forces the applicant to self-criticize within a dynamic in which they prefer to remain positive about their own abilities. Negative balance inquiries help protect the interviewer from being unduly influenced by continual exposure to only positive information from the candidate. Here's how the use of this negative balance inquiry typically works:

"Tell me about a time you disappointed your boss."

Long silence. "Oh, wow. That's a tough one. I mean, I am really good at what I do, and I think my boss would tell you that. I work hard. I take pride in doing a good job. I can't think of anything, really."

Note: When I ask attendees at my conferences, a number that is rapidly approaching half a million people, if they have ever disappointed their boss, everyone raises their hand. Why? Because *everyone has disappointed their boss*!

It is important for you to remain silent and maintain eye contact, indicating to the interviewee that you are waiting for a response.

"I mean, no one is perfect, right?" Nervous giggle. "I am sure I must have missed the mark at some point, but I can't think of anything major."

You remain silent.

"I mean, I miss a lot of deadlines then lie about why and . . ."

Okay, you probably won't get that response; but eventually the smart applicant will admit to some minor misstep in their performance. The point is not to learn the misstep – everybody makes mistakes – but to listen to how they explain the details. Do they immediately blame their boss, co-workers, the customer, or some other source outside of themselves? This would indicate that the person has an external locus of control. It also predicts that the first time they make a mistake at your organization, they will likely blame you, co-workers, the customer, or something else. Individuals with an external locus of control are less likely to improve with coaching.

However, if the applicant describes what they learned from the mistake and how they improved as a result of it, you are witnessing an internal locus of control. Employees with an internal locus of control take responsibility for their behaviors and are accountable for the outcomes of their work. They are more receptive to coaching and critical feedback. Just as important as a person's skills is this orientation. Peak performance cultures are built on an internal locus of control.

NEW HIRE ONBOARDING/ORIENTATION

Here's a couple of scary statistics for you. Remember that statistic in Chapter 2, "Horizontal Alignment," from *Employee Benefit News* – the one citing the cost of losing an employee as about 33 percent of their annual salary? Turns out, that's only half the story. The Society for Human Resources Management (SHRM) reports that the cost of hiring a new employee to replace an existing opening is 50–60 percent of that position's annual salary. Translated, if you are replacing an employee whose salary is $50,000.00, the total expense, including lost production, recruiting, and selection efforts, will cost as much as $30,000.00! And while that alone is daunting, it's only part of the challenge. Newly hired employees quit jobs at a rate of 30 percent of the time before the 90-day review, according to a study by jobvite.com (Job Seeker Nation Study, https://www.jobvite.com/wp-content/uploads/2018/04/2018_Job_Seeker_Nation_Study.pdf).

Combined, that indicates that companies are investing more than half of a new hire's annual salary into a process that will need to be repeated within three months nearly one-third of the time. That's equivalent to buying three cars and expecting one of the three to be replaced within three months with no trade-in value at all. That's crazy! There is no way you'd think that was reasonable, and we're talking about cars, not people. The impact on your organization's reputation as an employer in the community and the impact of morale within the organization are also being damaged in ways that are hard to quantify.

The Job Seeker Nation Study pointed out a few common reasons for the new hire's rapid departure:

- 43 percent say that the day-to-day role wasn't what they expected.
- 34 percent reported an incident or bad experience drove them away.
- 32 percent cite company culture as a reason for leaving.

All these reasons are cause for concern. I also think they are symptomatic of another barrier that new hires experience within the first 90 days: they feel stupid and uncomfortable.

Onboarding and orientation programs, together with the skills training discussed later, are about more than familiarizing a new employee with the organization's policies and procedures. Transitioning a new hire into the organization involves reducing their anxiety and ignorance related to beginning a job. Remember every human's four intrinsic needs: appreciation, independence, security, and options. It is unlikely when we start a new job that we experience much appreciation, independence, or options from our employer initially, since we are unable to contribute much to merit those rewards. That leaves security as the only intrinsic need that can be fulfilled early in our employment experience. Even if that intrinsic need isn't normally that important to the new hire, it is all we can offer at this point to instill motivation. The faster we can make the employee feel secure, the more time we buy ourselves to provide the training and opportunities for them to receive other intrinsic rewards.

The biggest challenge facing any organization as it relates to onboarding and orientation is achieving the commitment from all departments to its importance. Operationally, the organization is under pressure when there is a job opening. The new hire represents the eventual solution to this pressure. Consequently, the leader and members of the new hire's department are eager to get this person into the job and contributing. This eagerness often creates a desire to throw the new hire "into the fire," so to speak. Adding to this scenario is the likelihood that the orientation process is handled by another department like human resources, which schedules the meeting based on demand – say, once a month. The result is that the new hire often starts their job days or weeks before they have been oriented to the organization and responses to their questions are often some version of "You'll learn about that in orientation." Meanwhile, no intrinsic needs are being met.

A newly hired employee is experiencing a sort of variation of Maslow's Hierarchy of Needs. For them, it is essential that they feel sufficiently oriented to their surroundings before they can be comfortable performing job duties. To throw them into their job duties without a full understanding of more basic issues (where is the bathroom, when do I get paid, whom do I call if I am sick, etc.) will result in failure, reduced confidence, and increased anxiety. Eventually, they quit.

Smaller organizations have their own set of challenges. Many have no formal orientation program at all. New hires often sit down with a "buddy" or their manager who go over a set of topics organized as loosely as a checklist or worse. In some ways, this scenario is better than the delayed formal orientation situation. At least the new hire has a point of contact for questions and, if done thoroughly, should be armed with more knowledge. The key is that the process is formalized and comprehensive. No matter the organization's size, an employee handbook and formal onboarding process are essential.

For long-time employees, the employee "journey" has become routine. For a new hire, however, the employee journey is unfamiliar. Unlike our efforts to shepherd a customer through our process – aided by signage, assistance, and merchandising – the employee is often left to their own devices to make this journey correctly. Furthermore, it can be hard for long-time employees to remember all the things that were important to an employee on their first day.

For this reason, the best resource for constructing an employee journey map will always be new employees. No matter the size of your organization, an important part of the orientation should be obtaining feedback on the employee journey and how effective the company was at preparing the employee to navigate it. Here are a few things that people asked me in orientation (often privately) that were frequently not covered in any manuals:

- When do I get paid and how does that work?
- Where is the bathroom?
- Whom do I notify if I need a specific office supply?
- When does the schedule get posted?
- How do I request time off?
- What are all my benefits and how do they work?
- Where do I park?
- What is your attendance policy?
- Is there a list of all the departments? Organizational chart? Co-workers?
- What do I do if I need to call in sick, or I'm going to be late?
- Will I get business cards?

What struck me is that many of the questions are ones that might be uncomfortable for a new person to bring up with their boss because they involve taking time off or receiving perks/benefits. Truth is, we are often uncomfortable asking these questions for fear of looking bad. Still, the lingering discomfort of not knowing answers to these questions can contribute to the new hire leaving within the first 90 days.

The best onboarding and orientation programs require a comprehensive and honest discussion of all the topics potentially on a new hire's mind. The best way to know what those topics are is to ask the new hire directly and/or obtain the input from recent new hires who are more confident in providing you forthright answers to the question "When you started here, what do you wish we would have told you that we didn't?"

SKILLS TRAINING

Skills training is simultaneously the most obvious and overlooked element of the employee experience. For roles that allow for novices to learn on the job, most organizations have implemented some form of skills training to allow the new hire to achieve a level of mastery necessary to succeed on the job. This ranges from offline training that allows new hires to practice without risk of impacting the customer experience, to buddy systems and apprenticeships that provide opportunities for veteran employees to mentor their rookie co-workers. Whatever technique your organization employs to ensure that a new team member has developed the skills to succeed on the job, there are two considerations that will contribute to peak performance: efficacy metrics and self-efficacy support.

Skills training metrics means that you have some device to measure the new hire's ability to perform the job duties. This can be tough to achieve. For some tasks, like point of sale system training, you can design programs that challenge new hires to process various types of transactions and evaluate them for accuracy. For more conceptual tasks, you can design hypothetical scenarios to test new hires' knowledge of policies and procedures. With some creativity, nearly all the elements of a job description can be measured in a controlled environment. The key, as mentioned in Chapter 3, "Vertical Alignment," is that you have a well-designed job description. With that foundation, you can create various approaches to testing the new hire's capacity to perform each task.

No matter how thorough your skills training and efficacy metrics are, you will still find that the new hire struggles in the actual job initially. That was one of my biggest frustrations as a training manager in the corporate world. I would spend a week with employees preparing them to succeed on the retail sales floor, observing their success in the classroom and using metrics to confirm competency, only to be told by their supervisor that they didn't know what to do when they handled real transactions. I remember thinking that it was like the new hires got mental vapor lock when they hit the sales floor. It turns out, I was right. The problem wasn't that these individuals were incompetent. They were lacking in self-efficacy.

Self-efficacy is the feeling "I got this." Athletes refer to it as being "in the zone." Others have called it flow. Essentially, it is a combination of being competent at a task *and* feeling confident that you can handle it in the context you currently find yourself. The new hires I trained were competent, but they were not confident. And no amount of classroom education could completely prepare them for the introduction of real people with situations that were just different enough from the training examples to keep the new hire off balance.

The moral here is that no amount of skills training will ensure that a new hire will be effective initially unless paired with a situation that bolsters their confidence as they first practice these skills in a live setting. All new hires will need resources – in the form of both supportive co-workers and job aids – to help them apply what they learn in controlled settings.

The bottom line: organizations that achieve peak performance are dedicated to delivering skills training that builds the employee's competency and confidence. Doing so requires that the training conducted in controlled settings is measured for effectiveness *and* that there is a system for transitioning the employee from the classroom to the "real world" that builds their comfort level and results in self-efficacy.

CONTINUOUS COACHING AND PERFORMANCE FEEDBACK

Full disclosure as it relates to this aspect of the employee experience: I am befuddled by performance appraisal systems. Bear with me as I try to explain my angst and understand that I could write an entire book just covering my irritations relative to the performance appraisal process.

Of all the components of human resources management for which I have been responsible, the two most frustrating were employee recruiting and selection and performance feedback. As for the former, I still have night terrors originating from a period in my career that is nearly thirty years old. At that time in Central Florida, it was extremely challenging to find qualified candidates to fill openings in the hospitality industry. Combine that with turnover rates that routinely approached 80 percent and you'd find yourself in a lot of executive meetings facing the unpleasant glare of understaffed and overworked leaders pleading for relief. It was so frustrating knowing how many openings needed filling and not being able to locate talent. It was even more frustrating to learn that many of these openings need not have occurred at all, since our exit interviews administered to employees leaving our company often indicated that the reason for their departure was often avoidable. If only we had engaged in continuous coaching and performance feedback.

And so it was that one of my most frustrating issues birthed the other. To stem the tide of employees departing our company, I turned my attention to employee retention. "If we can't find good talent then we damn sure better hold on to the ones we have," I told myself. Excellent advice. Just like retaining customers in sales helps ease the burden of finding new business, retaining employees removes the pressure to continually find new ones. It's a simple concept. It was with this in mind that I set about revamping our performance appraisal system.

One of my critical thinking flaws is the tendency to accept an existing system and set out to fix it. Rather than take a step back and consider the merits of a process in general, I tend to accept the need for something and focus on improving it. It was this weakness that propelled me down a rabbit hole while trying to fix our performance appraisal system.

To understand what follows, let me outline the current approach we were using. It was a common system, revolving around an annual performance review document that included several generic appraisal metrics worded vaguely enough to generally apply to all the diverse jobs within the organization. Each metric was measured using a Likert scale that included "Unsatisfactory, Below Standards, Meets Standards, Above Standards, Outstanding." Each of those were assigned a numeric value of 1–5, respectively. Individuals who scored an overall average of 3.0 or higher with no single area scoring below 3.0 received an annual increase. Individuals scoring higher than 4.0 received a better increase. If you scored below 3.0 in any area, you were placed on a performance plan and required to improve to avoid further counseling.

On the surface, it seemed like a simple, effective system. Unfortunately, upon inspecting the annual reviews in employee files, I discovered some serious problems. Many leaders were providing little evidence to support their ratings. It was clear to me that many leaders invested very little time and thought when completing the review. As you would expect, many employees did not find the performance appraisal process to be meaningful or, worse yet, often discovered some criticisms of their performance for the first time during the review conversation. This would be poor form alone; but when you consider that the amount of their pay increase was contingent on their performance appraisal scores, it was also an affront to their pocketbook. Imagine doing your job for a year without hearing of any concerns about your performance, only to have the news that you weren't performing as expected sprung on you the moment your raise depends on it.

There was also evidence that leaders were inflating scores either to avoid confrontation with employees or to acquire a better pay increase for them – just like my example with Mateo and Jed a few chapters back. The former is evidence of poor leadership; the latter represents falsifying a company document for the purpose of inappropriately directing company monies (a fancy word for theft). So, in a nutshell, after reviewing the current state of our performance appraisal system, it appeared that a large percentage of our leaders didn't care about it, were afraid to use it correctly, and/or falsified the documents to inflate performance for the purposes of misappropriating company resources. Ugh.

What happens next is evidence of my unfortunate tendency to try to fix a system that really needed to be blown up and replaced completely. I tried to add more details to the existing document that would provide leaders with an easier process for matching the employee's performance to the language of the review. Basically, I tried to write the comments *for* the leaders so all they had to do was check the right box. Somehow, I thought the problem was that the leaders did not know how to define each of the five ratings on the Likert scale. I reasoned that if I were to provide a more comprehensive definition for each of the ratings, then the leaders would be more likely to rate employees accurately and have appropriate conversations with them.

That was a stupid assumption. The common term for my approach is "enabling." All I had done was to make it easier for the leaders to check a box rather than put some true thought into the employee's contribution. It was actually worse than the original process. I had many successes in human resources development during my decade-plus in the corporate world. This was not one of them.

Over the next 30 years, I have struggled to identify a perfect performance appraisal system. I have, however, learned a ton about what constitutes an effective one. Here are the descriptors for a performance feedback system for peak performance:

- It is **continuous**. It does not occur once a year, quarter, or month, but rather every day.
- It is **part of the culture**. This means that feedback – positive and critical – is expected.
- Performance is **viewed forward**, not backward. This means that we focus on goals and make developmental plans rather than evaluate history. Counseling deals with history.
- Performance discussions **link directly to job descriptions** to maintain vertical alignment.

- **Pay increases** are not linked to a document but rather to an **established range** that quantifies the value of the job to the organization and considers the performance of the employee within that range.

That last one is important and a little complicated. Here's the approach I like:

- Establish the minimum and maximum value for each job title in the organization. Minimum value would be the entry salary for a person with no experience; maximum value would be the highest salary you would be willing to pay someone to do this job. For example, let's say you have an opening for a tasting room manager at a small production winery. If you promoted someone to the position with no previous experience as a tasting room manager, you would extend the minimum salary (let's say $40,000 annually). If you recruited a seasoned tasting room manager from a competitor who was considered one of the best in the area wine industry, you might offer the maximum salary (let's say that is $60,000 annually). Your salary range for the tasting room manager job title is $40,000 to $60,000 annually.
- Establish three subranges within the range from minimum to maximum. Using the tasting room manager example, this range might be $40,000–$45,000 (low range); $45,000–$55,000 (mid-range); $55,000–$60,000 (high range). Note that the mid-range is larger than the low and high ranges.
- Merit increases are larger for high-performing individuals in the low range, smaller for those in the high range. This reflects the importance of rewarding high performers quickly so that they move into the mid-range rapidly. Once they have achieved the mid-range salary, high performers will experience declining merit increases that reflect the fact that they are rapidly reaching the maximum value this position offers the organization. Individuals in the high range may

receive only cost of living increases or small merit increases as they approach the maximum value this job has to the organization.

- This range should be adjusted annually based on cost of living (often around 2 percent) and competitive surveys.

The beauty of this system is that while experience is initially rewarded, performance will quickly reconcile inequities. If you are hired at a lower rate than a peer with more experience and you perform at a high level, you will rapidly close that gap. This system also encourages people to chart a career path that can move them to a new job title with a higher salary range – a process that feeds the career pathing process discussed below.

Coaching is every bit as important to employee performance and satisfaction as performance feedback. Clearly based on my angst and efforts, a lot of an organization's attention is routinely placed on installing a comprehensive performance appraisal process, and that's good. But the daily interactions between the leader and the team member are far more likely to provide the foundation for the employee experience. The problem is, coaching is much more organic, in the moment, fleeting and hard to quantify than performance appraisal. Rare is the organization that makes ongoing coaching techniques a focal point of their leadership development.

There are several approaches to coaching, and a leader's interactive style (Romantic, Warrior, Expert, or Mastermind) will affect how they execute it. Here are things to keep in mind when encouraging your leaders to engage in continuous coaching:

- Coaching involves both positive reinforcement for behaviors that reflect excellence and critical feedback when behaviors fall below standards.
- Coaching should be happening daily. If you haven't identified behaviors for praise or improvement every day, you are failing to provide continuous feedback.

- You cannot coach in solitude. Great leaders spend time with employees either in person, by phone, or by using the myriad technologies available to us (if leading remotely).
- Be mindful of the team member's intrinsic needs when coaching. As we discussed in Chapter 4, "Leadership Ideology," Romantics like appreciation, Warriors like independence, Experts like security, and Masterminds like options.
- Remember the wise words of Steve Thompson at PrimeLending: "Assume good intentions." When providing criticism, approach the employee with the assumption that they want to do good work and either don't know what to do or just made a poor decision. Few people are willfully bad at their job. One of my favorite ways to start a coaching session that involves a critical component is to say, "Help me understand why you did that." The employee's answer can provide tremendous insight into their thought process and allow you to give more meaningful guidance. In fact, on more than one occasion, I found myself thinking, "I would have done the same thing."
- Use benevolent accountability, as discussed in Chapter 4, to shift the responsibility for substandard performance from leader to team member over time.
- Reinforce an internal locus of control should the employee start blaming co-workers, the customer, or company policies for below-standard performance.
- Don't forget to employ a people preventative maintenance system as discussed in Chapter 4. It is important that coaching conversations are two-way systems that allow the team member to provide feedback about their experience to their leader. There is a reason that employees are referred to as internal customers. Don't lose sight of that.

Designing and applying a consistent process for continuous coaching, performance feedback and equitable and responsible compensation strategy are essential to peak performance.

CAREER PATHING

When you establish an effective performance feedback system – complete with forward-looking developmental plans, combined with a compensation system that encourages team members to continually evaluate future opportunities to increase their value to the organization – career pathing becomes self-propelling. In addition to these components of the employee experience, I recently heard some simple but profound advice from Karen Hedine, CEO of the local Walla Walla YMCA.

The Y in Walla Walla is not your typical gym. It is an integral part of the local community, providing community wellness, youth programs, child development, and social responsibility services through an expansive facility in the heart of wine country. The demographics of the area are broad and diverse. Like the Y, Karen is atypical as a leader. She came to nonprofit leadership having concluded a successful career leading organizations in the medical devices industry. When we sat down to construct a leadership development series for her team, she said something that resonated with me.

"Your job as a leader is to develop your replacement."

I had heard similar advice many times; but the matter-of-fact way that Karen said it – the simplicity and offhandedness of her tone –stopped me dead. I was jotting down notes of our conversation and wrote the sentence verbatim. I even underlined it twice. "That's it," I thought to myself. "That's the definition of leadership." It also aligns perfectly with the previously mentioned approach to recruiting and selection.

Not all employees want a career within the organization, but all employees want to be better by having been a part of it. If all leaders approached employee development as an exercise in preparing their team members for their next challenge, I can guarantee they would create a peak performance culture.

In the process of creating forward-looking developmental plans, team members will often share their longer-term aspirations. This could be career oriented, skills based, or interest based. Some employees think in terms of specific jobs – whether within or outside the organization – that they would like to pursue. Others focus on a skill that they would like to master, while others are intrigued simply by the chance to be exposed to new information. A peak performance culture provides resources to satisfy all these desires through a range of solutions. Tuition reimbursement, guest speaker series, lunch and learn workshops, and job shadowing programs are all great examples of an organization encouraging employees to explore their dreams.

A leader in a peak performance organization can answer this question off the top of her head: "What are the career aspirations of each member of your team?"

THE EMPLOYEE/CUSTOMER LINK

If passion is the foundation, alignment is the framework, and leadership ideology is the power, then both the employee and customer experience reflect the need to satisfy those who frequent our organization. They inhabit it – with different perspectives – and their fulfillment will determine our success. Great organizations never waver in their commitment to both of these populations and are continually evaluating their service delivery mediums to ensure that these critical elements of the success scoreboard are happy. They also understand that they are forever linked. Peak performance hinges on customer satisfaction, which hinges on employee satisfaction, which is created by exceptional leadership ideology, horizontal and vertical alignment, and a foundation in passion.

Key Considerations

- The employee experience directly impacts the customer experience. It is impossible to have satisfied customers if you have unsatisfied employees.

- Journey mapping is just as important for evaluating the employee experience as it is for customers. The process is different, however. While customers experience the organization in a linear, transactional flow, the employee has a systemic relationship with the company.

- The employee experience is most influenced by five factors: recruiting and selection, onboarding and orientation, skills training, continuous coaching and performance feedback (including compensation), and career pathing. How would employees rate each of the factors in your organization?

- Follow the recruiting and selection checklist to reduce the duration of job openings and enhance the likelihood that the new hire is the most qualified candidate.

- The single most influential personal quality that predicts a new hire's success is an internal locus of control.

- More employees leave within their first 90 days than at any other time. Be sure that you have a comprehensive onboarding, orientation, and skills training program to quickly make new employees comfortable.

- Skills training in controlled settings are important for the new employee's competency, but it doesn't address self-efficacy, an equally important component to performance. Make sure your skills training program has provisions for increasing the new-hire employee's confidence.

- Exceptional coaching and performance feedback systems are continuous and forward looking.

- Your job as a leader is to develop your replacement.

Chapter 7 It's Go Time!

I am betting that you are feeling a bit overwhelmed by all of this. Heck, after reading this book about 20 times during writing it, I am overwhelmed by it, too. There is a lot to get your head around. Who knew that creating a peak performance culture and operational excellence would be so much work? Ha! Well, put that way, of course we did. If it were easy, every organization would be the embodiment of peak performance. Yet few are.

Here's my recommendation. It is likely that some things really jumped out as priorities as you read about the importance of passion, core ideologies, vertically aligned practices, leadership ideologies, and the customer and employee experiences. You may have mumbled under your breath, "Yeah, we don't do that." Maybe you jotted down a particularly important point as you read. These may be the best indicators of where to start, although I would still encourage you to perform the full Peak Performance Culture Assessment.

When I was a kid, my dad knew it was better to keep me busy than allow me to fill an idle mind with mischief. He put me to work each summer starting at 12 years old to keep me from wandering the streets of my small hometown. When he caught me loafing, he would say, "Do something, even if it's wrong." Even today, my lovely bride understands that I do better when I have a task. At parties, I am the bartender or the dishwasher. When the host tries to make me stop, Lori jumps in to say, "He's better when he has a job."

Organizational development is the perfect foil for someone like me. There is always something to do. If you are wondering right now where to start, I suggest channeling my father. Pick something that feels off – misaligned, misexecuted, or just missed. Start working on making it better. The beautiful thing about organizational development is that it works exactly like Whack-a-Mole. Once you think you have hit the mark, another issue will pop up.

It would be great to start with a blank canvas, do market research, identify your success scoreboard, and construct a core ideology of vision, mission, and strategy that is horizontally aligned. From there, you could begin the daunting task for vertical alignment, perhaps by planning the human resources needs and creating job descriptions for positions. Next might come the employee handbook, sales and marketing strategies, and marketing materials. Leadership training would follow soon after and include time spent on customer journey mapping. The entire customer and employee experience would be examined, too. Oh, what a wonderful process this would be. But never has that ever happened in my life.

Also great, although a bit messier, is that you would gather together the executive leadership team and spend a day discussing the Peak Performance Culture Assessment that follows this chapter. That's bound to be a spirited and lengthy conversation. From that document, priorities can be identified, approaches agreed upon, and actions undertaken. That's a far more common methodology for organizational development work and one that I endorse wholeheartedly.

More likely, you just jump in. Organizational development is messy and achieving a peak performance culture means that you start from some degree of underperformance. That's okay. Even if your efforts don't succeed, you will learn a lot about what you need to do now. We always learn more from our failures than our successes. Success can be luck; failure never is.

The important part is to start. As Dad's saying reinforces, nothing gets done until you start. Besides, his saying had a second, more important point:

"Do something, even if it's wrong. It is easier to fix a mistake than a regret."

Appendix: Peak Performance Culture
The Five Metrics of Organizational Excellence

The Peak Performance Culture Assessment is meant to provide guidance into an examination of the current state of the organization's culture, provoke thought into a desired future state that improves the organization, and identify action items (initiatives, strategies, tasks, tactics, etc.) that will move the organization from where it is today to where we want it to be in the future.

The assessment is best administered with a leadership team. Due to its comprehensive nature, it is appropriate to complete the evaluation in multiple settings. The most common methodology for completing the assessment is to utilize five separate meetings, each focusing on one of the individual metrics: **horizontal alignment, vertical alignment, leadership ideology, customer experience,** and **employee experience.** This allows for organizations to work on each metric before moving on to the next. While peak performance is not a strictly linear concept, organizations that are horizontally aligned are more likely to achieve more effective vertical alignment. Solid vertical alignment promotes better leadership ideology, which promotes enhanced customer and employee experiences.

PEAK PERFORMANCE CULTURE ASSESSMENT

Cultural Component	Current State	Desired Future State	Action Item(s)
Horizontal Alignment			
Knowledge of market environment			
Mechanism for ongoing evaluation of market environment			
Clearly defined success scoreboard			
Core ideology that connects market environment with success scoreboard			

Cultural Component	Current State	Desired Future State	Action Item(s)
Vertical Alignment			
Our core ideology is a driving force in determining our brand and culture.			
The job descriptions provide a vehicle to achieve vertical alignment.			
We have a comprehensive employee handbook that outlines organization-wide policies and procedures.			
Our organization-wide practices match our expressed policies and procedures.			
All divisions, locations, and departments apply the organization-wide procedures the same.			
All individuals in the organization know and reflect our core ideology.			
Our customers experience our core ideology from the sales process to the product/service delivery.			

Cultural Component	Current State	Desired Future State	Action Item(s)
Leadership Ideology			
We hire character, train skills, and lead style.			
The organization manifests, instills, and rewards an internal locus of control among the employee base.			
The organization empowers employees and reconciles the imbalance between authority and impact.			
High-value employees receive leadership training in advance of being placed in management roles.			
The organizational environment provides for the intrinsic needs of the employees.			
Employees are trained in the skill of conflict resolution and practice dialectic thinking.			
Leaders utilize "zero-based thinking" in evaluating all elements of the operation.			
Employee counseling utilizes a system of shifting accountability from leader to team member.			
The organization has a system for people preventative maintenance.			
The organization displays exceptional seamwork.			

Cultural Component	Current State	Desired Future State	Action Item(s)
Customer Experience			
The organization displays a "servant's heart."			
The organization has an effective client advisory board.			
The organization has an effective client advocacy council.			
The customer journey has been mapped and includes all critical interactions.			
The customer experience will appeal to a broad range of customer styles.			
The organization has a device for measuring customer satisfaction and loyalty.			
The customer experience is prioritized over operational efficiency.			
The organization displays an effective service recovery process for unsatisfied customers.			

Cultural Component	Current State	Desired Future State	Action Item(s)
Employee Experience			
The organization has a device for measuring employee satisfaction and loyalty.			
The organization has a well-designed recruiting and selection process.			
The organization has a well-designed onboarding and orientation process.			
Employees receive effective skills training.			
The organization executes a continuous coaching and performance feedback system.			
All employees have a career path and developmental plan.			
Other considerations not addressed above.			

ONGOING ENHANCEMENT

Completing and implementing the results of the Peak Performance Culture Assessment is best viewed as an ongoing, continuous process of organization enhancement. While there is a distinct starting point, there is rarely an end. The key is to establish current states, desired future states, and priorities for initiatives. Also keep in mind that high-level initiatives – like those that occur within horizontal and vertical alignment – will have a significant impact on leadership ideology, customer experience, and employee experience. In that same vein, issues identified in leadership ideology, customer experience, and employee experience may be rooted in horizontal and/or vertical alignment.

One final consideration. As the book makes clear, peak-performing cultures are built on a foundation of passion. Passion must be prevalent at the executive leadership level for an organization to reach its full potential. Any self-assessment of peak performance must begin with a frank and honest exploration of the level of passion at the highest leadership levels. Are executives deriving sufficient joy from the work? Without joy, there is no passion, and no amount of desire can sustain performance sufficiently to compensate for this. Spend some time talking with executives about passion (joy in action over an enduring period) to determine if the foundation for peak performance is in place.

HORIZONTAL ALIGNMENT ASSESSMENT

(Refer to Chapter 2)

Horizontal alignment involves the development of a core ideology (vision, mission, strategy) that links the current market environment (inputs) with a success scoreboard (profitability/fiscal solvency, operational efficiency, and stakeholder satisfaction). It is an essential metric of a peak-performing culture.

After reading Chapter 2 in this book, schedule a meeting to engage in horizontal alignment. Consider beginning this meeting with a team building activity to encourage open and respectful interaction throughout the process. Also, performing a basic SWOT analysis on the current state of the organization will help with many of these discussion areas.

Discussion questions:

- How would you describe the general market for our products and services?
- Who are our most formidable competitors and why?

- Who are our customers?
- Why would a customer choose us versus our competitors?
- Why would a customer choose our competitors versus us?
- Are there any issues specific to the location of our business/branches that we should consider (local demographics, legislation, taxes, etc.)?
- What emerging trends do we expect to impact our business?
- What level of profitability do we wish to achieve?
- How will we measure operational efficiency?
- Do we have a process for continuous improvement of our operations?
- How will we know if our ownership is satisfied?
- How will we measure customer satisfaction?
- What are the elements of our products/services that promote loyalty and retention among our customers? Do they exist in both abundance and consistency?
- How will we measure employee satisfaction?
- What are the elements of employment that promote loyalty and retention among our employees? Do they exist in both abundance and consistency?
- As an organization, do we need to go in a new direction (aspirational – a new "secret sauce") or refine our current direction (reflective – use our current "secret sauce")?
- What is our vision (desired future state)?
- How would you compare the current state of the organization to our desired future state?
- What is the most important differentiator(s) between us and our competitors (mission) that can move us from our current state to our desired future state (vision)?
- How can we apply our mission (strategy) to achieve our vision?
- What is our core ideology (vision, mission, strategy)?

VERTICAL ALIGNMENT ASSESSMENT

(Refer to Chapter 3)

Vertical alignment is both critical and daunting as it relates to organizational excellence. It is an ongoing process and requires the installation of devices for the continuous evaluation and aligning of all operations, policies, and procedures at every level of the organization. Identifying misalignment is extremely important. Equally so is having a mechanism for evaluating all processes moving forward. As explained in the book, a few areas are especially enlightening when evaluating vertical alignment: job descriptions, sales processes, and the brand promise. By focusing on these, you can begin identifying misalignments. Aligning these will uncover more misalignments and so forth.

Finally, consider performing a TOWS analysis to provide a deeper understanding of how the organization's strengths, weaknesses, opportunities, and threats impact vertical alignment.

Discussion questions:

- Do we have an employee handbook? Is it comprehensive?
- Do all divisions/departments apply the policies in the handbook consistently?
- Does every job title have an accompanying job description?
- Do the job descriptions include the eleven elements outlined in Chapter 6, "The Employee Experience"?
- Do the job descriptions support alignment in the nine key organization-wide processes discussed in Chapter 6?
- Is the organization's core ideology represented in its interactions with customers and employees?
- Does the sales process align with the core ideology?
- Does the sales team believe the organization delivers on the core ideology?
- Do all of our employees know our core ideology? If not, why?
- What practices exist at the organization, divisional/departmental, or individual level that are aligned and are

strengths? How do we leverage these to best take advantage of our opportunities? How do we use these to protect against threats?

- What practices exist at the organization, divisional/ departmental, or individual level that are clearly misaligned? Why are these occurring? How will better aligning these practices better position us to take advantage of our opportunities? How can we reduce our threats by better aligning these practices?

LEADERSHIP IDEOLOGY ASSESSMENT

(Refer to Chapter 4)

Defining an organization's leadership ideology is similar to establishing its core values. Both involve identifying the characteristics that the entire employee base should manifest to translate the core ideology from the words that explain the vision, mission, and strategy into a daily set of behaviors that will make them real, tangible, competitive differentiators. The best leadership ideologies share some qualities – those outlined below and described throughout the book. These provide an exceptional starting point for evaluating your peak performance potential. Be aware: this discussion among a leadership team requires honest, thoughtful interactions and can test the mettle of even the most effective groups.

Discussion questions:

- Do we live by the tenet "hire character, train skills, lead style"?
- Do we as a team and as an organization understand the meaning of "internal locus of control"? Do we exhibit it in all our interactions with one another and the customer?
- How do we currently ensure we hire individuals with an internal locus of control?

- How do we use empowerment to reconcile the imbalance of influence – leadership authority, line level impact – within the organization?
- Is mid-level leadership sufficiently trained and supported to balance influence?
- Does the organization culture have ample levels of intrinsic rewards for all types of performers: appreciation, independence, security, and flexibility?
- Do we resolve conflict in a healthy way?
- Do we train our employees on dialectic thinking and conflict resolution skills?
- Do we apply a zero-based thinking approach to employee performance? To operational processes and decision making?
- Do our leaders assume full responsibility for performance deficiencies among our team or systems?
- Do we quickly engage in a process to correct performance deficiencies and shift accountability from leadership to team member?
- Do we have a continuous, preemptive process for collecting data on the employee engagement before issues become toxic (people preventative maintenance system)?
- How do we respond to critical feedback from our employees?
- How strong are the "seams" in our organization?
- Do we have a strategy for strengthening organizational seamwork?

CUSTOMER EXPERIENCE ASSESSMENT

(Refer to Chapter 5)

Virtually every organization places a high priority on customer satisfaction, but few effectively translate their intentions into an exemplary customer experience. The reasons for this can range from complacency to a lack of awareness of what matters to customers. With changing customer expectations and increased competition, static processes and uninspired employees can quickly diminish the customer experience and create a loss of retention. This has the effect of burdening the business development function with the daunting task of replacing revenues with new clients. All peak-performing organizations exhibit a "servant's heart" – a fundamental desire to understand and fulfill the needs of their customers.

Discussion questions:

- Do we utilize a formal customer service training program? Describe it.
- How effective is our mechanism for measuring customer satisfaction?
- How do we collect information about client loyalty and retention?
- Do we utilize client advisory boards and customer advocacy councils to encourage continuous client feedback loops?
- Have we performed customer journey mapping?
- What are the first five critical interactions between our organization and the client? Be prepared to list more than one set of five if your organization has multiple operational entry points (online versus physical location, for example), product/service lines, or geographic locations.
- Have we defined a neutral experience for each of these critical interactions?
- How could the organization create a positive experience for each of these critical interactions?
- Does our operation make use of the positive filtering phenomenon to establish an exceptional first impression?
- Does our customer experience address different client currencies – relationships, solutions, knowledge, and options?
- Describe the process for service recovery. Are employees trained to positively resolve a customer concern?

EMPLOYEE EXPERIENCE ASSESSMENT

(Refer to Chapter 6)

It is common for most organizations to place far greater importance and resources on the customer experience compared to the employee experience. Peak performance cultures, however, rightly view the two as indelibly linked. They know that behavior breeds behavior. As such, an organization's ability to deliver an exceptional customer experience is hamstrung by the degree to which it does the same for the employee experience. One simple question can be helpful as a starting point in evaluating the employee experience: "Do we place the same priority on our employees' experience as we do the customers'?"

Discussion questions:

- Describe the recruiting and selection process. Using the Recruiting and Selection Checklist in (Chapter 6), determine what gaps exist between the current state and a desired future state that includes all the elements in that checklist.
- Describe our new hire onboarding/orientation process.
- Describe our skills training program.
- Do new employees have a mechanism for providing feedback about the onboarding process?
- Do we have a mechanism for collecting feedback from employees about their experience?
- Have we completed an employee journey map and identified critical interactions?
- How do employees receive performance feedback?
- How do we determine employee initial compensation and performance pay increases?
- Do all employees have developmental plans and a career path?

About the Author

Dave Mitchell is an internationally recognized, award-winning speaker on leadership, relationships, selling skills, and customer experience. He founded the Leadership Difference, Inc. in 1995. His popularity is based on his unique ability to bring humor and authenticity to proven business strategies and complicated applied cognitive psychology concepts. He is also a certified advanced wine sommelier, which is a far more popular topic for discussion at parties. In addition to this book, Dave authored *Live and Learn or Die Stupid*, *The Power of Understanding People*, and *The Power of Understanding Yourself*.

When not traveling around the world delivering "enter-train-ment" to his many clients, Dave enjoys tending to 20 acres of land outside Walla Walla in the heart of the Washington wine country with his lovely bride, Lori. They have two adult children, Brooke and Slade, and a collection of animals of the equine, canine, and feline varieties.

Index